42 Rules for Creating WE

Edited by Judith E. Glaser
Foreword by Angela Ahrendts
CEO, Burberry Group PLC

E-mail: info@superstarpress.com
20660 Stevens Creek Blvd., Suite 210
Cupertino, CA 95014

Second Printing: November 2009
First Printing: July 2009
Paperback ISBN: 978-1-60773-048-4
Place of Publication: Silicon Valley, California, USA
Library of Congress Number: 2009932454

eBook ISBN: 978-1-60773-049-1

Trademarks

Warning and Disclaimer

Praise For This Book!

"One of the most pleasing and captivating aspects of music is the ability to identify and bring together sounds that when heard individually would appear lacking and discordant into a beautiful and complete harmony. In '42 Rules for Creating WE,' leaders will learn how to listen for these different sounds and how they can use them to bring about the harmonization of their organization into a beautiful and complete WE."
Nile Rodgers, CEO, We are Family Foundation; Composer; Music Producer

"'42 Rules of Creating We' presents a multi-dimensional philosophy regarding the creation of an organizational context in which profound insights into human nature and interrelationships can be harnessed for greater productivity, success and compatibility. This approach requires the exploration and adoption of concepts that are fundamental to the human condition such as truth, integrity, attitude and sensitivity to others and their ideas."
Kenneth Bistany, Past President, CPC International East Asia

"Even military organizations have to look beyond traditional norms and find ways to be inclusive and imaginative. Creating WE helps readers to tap into that intuitive wisdom we all possess, but have lost sight of in this competitive world."
Chief Warrant Officer 3 Michelle Criste, Instructional Systems School Chief

"In her groundbreaking work, *Creating We*, Judith E. Glaser provides a manual for building high functioning teams by focusing on the human characteristics that most often sabotage our best efforts at getting people to work together. Now through the collaboration of members of The Creating We Institute, she has put together additional recipes for success that provide 42 different insights into building a WE-centric organization. Like a cookbook, the 42 Rules can be read in any order depending on the occasion and background of the reader. You'll find helpful tools for any management style and a wide variety of situations."
Richard Naylor, MLS, MBA, Director of the William K. Sanford Town Library

"To create an environment where people can thrive and succeed is every leader's hope and goal. '42 Rules for Creating WE,' with its down to earth tips and tools, masterfully written by those who have spent decades building WE-Centric environments across the globe, is an immeasurably important contribution towards this end. Leaders will forever be thankful for having read it."
Damien Dernoncourt, CEO, John Hardy Limited

"One of the most powerful and profound leadership ideas I've encountered is WE-centric thinking. Fact is, the Gary Cooper go-it-alone heroic model did't even work in High Noon; he needed Grace Kelly's help to finish off the bad guys! Now, members of The Creating We Institute have written this very accessible book of 42 rules to help everyone shift from I-centric thinking to more inclusive, more productive ways of working and being with others. It is a guidebook to co-creating our futures, worth reading and keeping and reading again."
Joel Marks, Vice President/Executive Producer, Learning Communications

"To paraphrase Victor Hugo, 'Nothing is as powerful as an idea whose time has come.' Judith Glaser and fellow members of The Creating We Institute have created a highly original and thought-provoking book that is a strong affirmation of the power of WE—an idea whose time has come. The authors of '42 Rules for Creating WE' do a great job in demonstrating the power of WE-centric thinking and how it can help us create stronger families, communities, companies and nations."
Peggy Murrah and Chris Muccio, co-authors of 42 Rules for 24 Hour Success on LinkedIn

"'42 Rules' is a handy collection of relationship gems—whenever you feel stuck in a relationship and wonder how to get unstuck, pick up this treasure trove and find the gem of insight that provides a roadmap for getting unstuck."
Dr. Pierce J. Howard, author, The Owner's Manual for the Brain

For more testimonials and quotes for this book, please see "Additional Praise For This Book!" at the end of this book.

Foreword by Angela Ahrendts

I have always felt that when Judith Glaser and I met over 20 years ago, it was not simply by chance, but one of life's predestined gifts. I was in my first large leadership position as the President of Donna Karan and, in parallel, Judith had recently launched her new business venture. We connected at an inflection point in both of our careers, spending hours curiously delving into personal philosophies and methodologies while discovering that our joint energy and shared perspective resulted in intriguing insights. Many of her early lessons and insights are still part of my leadership style today.

When The Creating WE Institute was born two years ago, I had no doubt that this diverse group of highly accredited individuals would collectively create one of the most valuable leadership bibles for this generation. They united as a team to create the 'WE' they would write about, enacting, analyzing, and testing the *42 Rules* we would soon read.

As a modern-thinking, hands-on CEO of a PLC (Public Limited Company), I love that the themes contained in this work are centered on human emotions and instincts. We intuitively and informally use many of these rules numerous times a day and *42 Rules* helps to focus, organize, and magnify the importance of each, giving us further inspirational insights into how to more constructively and systematically leverage within our organizations.

In 2006, Burberry began its transformation from a private to a public company, revitalizing the company for a second time in 10 years while planning to double revenue and profits in five years—no easy feat. The estimated probability of success was five percent. We knew that a brilliant team of functional experts was our only possibility to achieve our goals; a team that would 'Shatter Old Paradigms,' and truly understand 'What Moves People' to perform at their peak.

We agreed early on that our course of action would not be what was best for the individual, but what was best for the brand. We all had to be selfless to win (Rule #3) and in order to build brand momentum, we knew we needed a focused, consciously contagious 'Cult Like Culture' that in itself would create the energy needed to permeate throughout the company—(Rule

#15). Along with passion and energy, our new team was built on a trust that allowed us to further 'Foster Integrity, Candor, and Caring.' We did not simply hire great individuals, but individuals who were culturally compatible with our organization and served as great team members.

As a global luxury brand in a fast-moving, socially-interconnected world, communication across all mediums was a critical component in clarifying a pure and consistent vision. We needed to be acutely aware of how a united, focused, sharing, synergistic team could achieve far greater things for our business, our employees, and the communities where we live and work (Rule #28; Rules #36-42) and that our Brand is our beacon to our employee, customer, and consumer constituencies worldwide. Indeed, our greatest accomplishment at Burberry has been to instill a strong faith or belief in the team, brand, and vision while always adhering to the lifelong golden rule, or as The Creating We Institute calls it, 'Walk In Their Shoes' (Rule #18), and maintaining a constant awareness of 'How Words Create Worlds.'

It took Napoleon Hill nearly 25 years to write his legendary guidebook for individual success, 'Think and Grow Rich.' Judith and The Creating WE Institute (with over a thousand years of combined experience) have written today's greatest guide for team success in less than two and it will soon be read by all Burberry employees worldwide. Just as Judith did over 20 years ago, this exceptional guidebook has arrived at the perfect time to help lead Burberry and myself even further toward achieving our dreams.

Angela Ahrendts, CEO
Burberry Group PLC
July, 2009

Dedication to my Creating WE Institute colleagues

Judith E. Glaser

In 2007, a friend and colleague, Peg Aldridge, asked if I would be interested in designing an innovation summit for Queens University in Charlotte, North Carolina. Within a few months, our Innovation Summit launched, and there were more than 300 attendees with 30 facilitators on hand for the two-day event. Out of this rippled an energy that has been unstoppable. I am forever grateful for Peg's influence in moving me to step up to this big and exciting challenge.

Next, a great thing happened—I got an email from South Africa from Louise van Rhyn—who I didn't yet know—to fly to South Africa and work with her to introduce my work to leaders from all walks of life. I couldn't say no to Louise. You will understand why when you read her 'Respond with Yes!' Rule. My two-week visit to South Africa brought me into conversation with thousands of leaders there, in business and government, as well as consultants, coaches and employees to discuss and explore my concepts, ideas and practices on Creating WE.

After our South African work, Louise wanted to come to the U.S. to become certified in Creating WE principles and practices, and I invited my 'thought leadership circle' of colleagues to join us. In October of 2007, I launched the first Creating WE **Thought Leadership Summit**.

A month before the Summit, a few of us (Jerry Manas, Peg Aldridge, Nancy Ring and I) created a virtual venue on the web to start conversations amongst people who hadn't yet met each other in person. An incredible curiosity soon emerged as people began to pose 'big questions' they wanted to discuss with others prior to the Summit. These included examining and understanding 'the connections between language, energy, and the neuroscience of relationships.'

Everyone was curious about what others had to say. The camaraderie within the group surfaced even before our face-to-face meeting, and the Summit far exceeded everyone's expectations. My colleagues developed deep connections and became a cohesive team. At the Summit we discussed big themes such as energy, neuroscience, branding, innovation, generativity and humanity. We discovered common bonds based on infusing a new spirit of WE into the world. We each shared what we were working on with clients, and how we were thinking and evolving our unique practice areas. During this deep sharing process we got excited about each other's passions.

At the end of our 2.5 days together, we unanimously agreed to form The Creating We Institute (CWI). Brian Penry, our resident Art Director and brand guru, created the incredible logo for us, which is on the cover of this book. In short order our Institute members started interacting with each other regularly. Over the course of the next six months we began co-authoring articles. When Ken Shelton's 'Executive Excellence' Magazine featured four of our articles (in the July 2008 issue) we thought we'd gone to heaven!

Finding our 'virtual' conversations—and our 'new voices' so exciting, we wanted more face time to 'co-create,' and so we held a second Summit. In the second Summit, we recognized that something was happening in the room: in co-creating and exploring new territory we had entered a 'generative' state, one we wanted to learn more about, and share with our clients.

We found we were becoming bolder, more innovative, and more open to new ways of thinking. We came up with a term for this new paradigm; terming the energy we felt with and for each other 'generative connectivity.' We also decided that we were becoming pioneers in an emerging field, one that we see as 'the neuroscience of WE.' We are also eagerly engaged in translating what we are learning in this emerging field into practical wisdom for leaders so they can help their organizations achieve higher levels of productivity and engagement.

The 'Creating WE Institute' has been structured to undertake research, writing projects, and client interventions. We are certifying others—clients—in our work so that they can learn what we are learning. We are developing TAGs (Targeted Action Groups) to engage practitioners and clients with similar interests in a structured way of co-developing tools to bring this work into organizations. We hope you will visit our website and read more about who we are and what we believe in—(www.creatingweinstitute.com) Please also reach out to us if you are inspired to be a part of the Institute—and the energy that is emerging around creating more 'WE' in the world!

Big Thank Yous!

I want to thank all of my colleagues at The Creating We Institute for taking an open-minded leap with me into new ways of thinking.

None of us knew when we started where this incredible journey would take us, but the energy and enthusiasm has just continued to grow and grow.

Creating We Institute - 2009 Active Members

www.creatingweinstitute.com

- Peg Esgate Aldridge
- Bud Bilanich
- Barbara Biziou
- Michelle Boos-Stone
- Dale Kramer Cohen
- Bruce Cryer (Board Member)
- Deborah Dumaine
- Jon Entine
- Bob Fuller
- Robert Galinsky
- Deborah E. Garand
- Lisa Giruzzi
- Judith E. Glaser
- Liz Glaser
- Richard Glaser
- Jan Goldstoff
- Geoff Grenert
- Elizabeth Hall
- Denise Harrington
- Lara Herscovitch

- Jane M. Hewson
- Charles Jones
- Rex E. Jung
- Stanley Labovitz
- Kate Grace MacElveen
- Jerry Manas
- Deborah Hicks Midanek
- Catherine Mullally
- Fernando Natalici
- Katinka Nicou
- Brian Penry
- Whitaker H. Raymond
- Donna Riechmann
- Nancy Ring
- Tom Rosenwald
- Mary Ann Somerville
- Cindy Tortorici
- Louise van Rhyn
- Josephine Washington

I also want to deeply thank our new colleagues and clients who have shown interest in drawing on our Institute and our body of work. With you, aboard, I know we can and *will* expand the capacity for leaders to grow and evolve their WE-centric leadership around the world!

And to my summer interns and editors Carla Rood and Rami Glatt—I couldn't have done this without you! Thank you so much for proofing the book and making sure we said what we wanted to say clearly! A special thanks too to my third intern, Anna Borgwing, who is also working with me to produce the Authors Studio Interviews, which I am doing with incredible leaders. And my fourth intern Yaakov Cohen, who is helping us organize our Neuro-tips which we will make available for those who want to better understand the science behind why Creating WE works.

Most importantly, a special thank you to our clients! For over 28 years these wonderful human beings that I have had the great privilege of working with have amazed me with their pioneering spirit, passion to learn, and their willingness to step into transformative 'experiments' with us to discover how powerful, phenomenal and resilient the human spirit truly is. This includes clients like Angela Ahrendts, CEO of Burberry, who wrote the Foreword for this book. She has been a mentor and teacher to so many generations of leaders, and has taught me about the power of believing in a vision.

And thank you to our other clients who have been willing to walk the path of discovering new ways of thinking with courage, with intelligence and with heart. They are the real teachers of this work, who have opened my eyes—our eyes—to what 'WE' in action really means.

The Creating WE Institute is young. We are still discovering our identity and our value in the world. In spite of this, what I know is that we are a group of talented, passionate, inspirational, and dedicated humanitarians. For all we have created thus far, and for the great promise of an exciting future, I am truly grateful.

Epigraph

"We do not believe in ourselves until someone reveals that deep inside us is valuable, worth listening to, worthy of our trust, sacred to our touch. Once we believe in ourselves we can risk curiosity, wonder, spontaneous delight or any experience that reveals the human spirit."

—E. E. Cummings (1894-1962), poet, playwright, painter, essayist

"We need to give each other the space to grow, to be ourselves, to exercise our diversity. We need to give each other space so that we may both give and receive such beautiful things as ideas, openness, dignity, joy, healing, and inclusion."

—Max De Pree (b.1924), author, former CEO of Herman Miller, Inc.

"There is no such thing as a 'self-made' man. We are made up of thousands of others. Everyone who has ever done a kind deed for us, or spoken one word of encouragement to us, has entered into the make-up of our character and of our thoughts, as well as our success."

—George Burton Adams (1851-1925), educator, historian

Contents

Foreword	Foreword by Angela Ahrendts v
Preface	Preface by Judith E. Glaser 1
Intro	Introduction. 5

Section I	**Shatter Old Paradigms 8**
Rule 1	Rules are Meant to Be Broken 10
Rule 2	There Is No Quid Pro Quo in WE 12
Rule 3	Be Selfish to Become Selfless 14
Rule 4	Live in Your Heart's Zone 16

Section II	**Acknowledge the 'I' Inside the 'WE' . . . 18**
Rule 5	There is an 'I' in Team 20
Rule 6	Speak from the 'I'—Listen from the 'WE' . . 22
Rule 7	Become a Creating WE Leader 24
Rule 8	Seek to Mine for Value. 26
Rule 9	Take Your Seat at the Table and Use It! . . . 28

Section III	**Understand What Moves People 30**
Rule 10	Create a Virtual Water Cooler 32
Rule 11	Living the Brand Creates WE 34
Rule 12	Harness Collective Wisdom 36

Rule 13 | Respond with "Yes!"...................38

Rule 14 | Sometimes Thinking Small
Has Big Payoffs......................40

Rule 15 | Be Consciously Contagious............42

Section IV | Foster Integrity, Candor and Caring .. 44

Rule 16 | The Torch of Integrity.................46

Rule 17 | Tell It Like It Is.......................48

Rule 18 | Walk in Their Shoes..................50

Rule 19 | Respect the Views of Your Adversary.....52

Rule 20 | Forgive and Not Forget.................54

Rule 21 | Act in a Manner That Honors Yourself
and Your Associates...................56

Rule 22 | Speak Your Vulnerable Truth............58

Rule 23 | Practice Presence.....................60

Section V | Understand When to Pull
Instead of Push...................62

Rule 24 | Move With, Not Against, Partners........64

Rule 25 | Seek Engagement, Not Compliance......66

Rule 26 | Listen to Connect.....................68

Rule 27 | Embrace Different Perspectives.........70

Rule 28 | Synergize Your Teams.................72

Section VI | Realize How Words Create Worlds ... 74

Rule 29 | Create Shared Meaning.................76

Rule 30 | Support Others in Recognizing Needs. . . . 78

Rule 31 | Separate Opinions from Facts 80

Rule 32 | Be Willing to Change Our Beliefs 82

Rule 33 | Advocate for Needs, Not Means 84

Rule 34 | We Are What We Write. 86

Rule 35 | Be Elegantly Inclusive 88

Section VII | Expand Belief Systems
and Perspectives 90

Rule 36 | Think and Act "BIG WE, little me" 92

Rule 37 | Trumpets for Success 94

Rule 38 | Look Back to Look Forward 96

Rule 39 | Look at WE, Not Me 98

Rule 40 | Focus On What Works. 100

Rule 41 | Create a Shared Vision for the Future . . . 102

Rule 42 | These are Our Rules. What are Yours? . . 104

Editor | About the Editor 106

Appendix A | Contributors' Background. 108

Appendix B | Tools, Resources & Assessments 128

Appendix C | Books 132

Appendix D | References 134

Your Rules | Write Your Own Rules 136

Books | Other Happy About Books 138

Preface by Judith E. Glaser

A few years ago, I invited nearly 40 colleagues to join me for what I called a Thought Leadership Summit. We didn't really have a plan in mind for how we wanted to work together, or even what that work would be; what we did have was the recognition of a special energy connecting our small group of talented colleagues. We all held an incredible level of respect for the unique values and skills each person brought to the table, and we felt comfortable talking with each other and exploring our deepest aspirations together.

Every day, whether it is for work or for life in general, we move in and out of relationships based on our needs and what others have to offer, or just simply because a job requires us to do so. However, during the first meeting of this new group of people, we discovered we were developing a very special relationship with each other, different from any we had ever experienced before. We found we had higher levels of empathy and connectivity than we normally did with others and wanted a way to cultivate this even further—and thus, The Creating We Institute was born.

At our second Summit, we spent time defining what had transpired at the first Summit. We ended up calling what we had experienced 'Generative Connectivity' and decided we wanted to write about it, share it and see how it integrated into our lives and our sense of well being.

Today, only a year and a half later, we are forging new alliances with each other and with new Creating WE Institute colleagues. We are always finding more people to invite to join us in our exploration of new and profound research around the neuroscience of WE, and in other related areas.

Executive Excellence Magazine: Ken Shelton, publisher of Executive Excellence magazine had the foresight to publish my first article on Vital Instincts, which correlates what happens at the cellular level in organisms to what happens at the organizational levels. Cancer in cells and cancer in organizations are mirror images. With Ken's continued support of the 'WE-centric' theme, my writing and now our writing has enabled us to advance our work and exploration to where we are today. August 2009 Executive Excellence magazine will publish a CWI Journal of articles on *Brain, Brand & Energy*. This will serve as a useful supplement to '42 Rules for Creating WE' for those who are seeking a greater understanding of the neuroscience underlying this book.

Mergers and Acquisitions: Since the writing of '42 Rules for Creating WE,' we have also been creating alliances with associations such as the Alliance of Mergers & Acquisitions, a national organization of lawyers, accounting firms, private equity executives and business people, and we are working on building assessment tools to help raise the success ratio for M & A's.

Neuroscience of WE Summit: In addition to publishing literature on the topic of applied neuroscience, we have developed a summit for leaders called Bring Neuro-innovation Back to Your Workplace. It's based on what we call 'The Wisdom of the 5 Brains,' and enables leaders to understand how our social brains work. By focusing on the neuroscience of WE our goal is to utilize current research in the field of neuroscience and make it accessible and useful to leaders by applying this wisdom to situations they often face at work such as how to: handle conflicts, run better meetings, execute strategies, harvest innovation and expand collaboration in business settings.

Reality TV: We've formed a partnership with Robert Galinsky, creator of Reality TV School. We are melding our talents to bring leaders an 'out of the chair' experience of how our brains work under pressure, under fire, and when we are in an optimum state of mind. In our program with the working title 'Reality TV Meets the Wisdom of the 5 Brains,' we are using innovative 'improvisational techniques' that create a powerful acceleration in how leaders can shift into higher levels of leadership presence. In this session we simulate conversations—called 'real plays'—so that leaders can see how conversations impact us when they emanate from each of our 5 brains.

Leaders get to see when our lower, less human brains are hijacking us and when we are speaking from our highest brain—and then learn to shift from lower to higher-level conversational skills.

Temple University and The Guru Nation: As part of the evolution of the Institute, we have created an alliance with the Dean of Temple University's School of Liberal Arts as well as the Dean of its School of Neuroscience. Our hope is to work with them in co-creating a Neuroscience Summit for 2010. To this end, we will be inviting Amy Dorn Kopelan, CEO of The Guru Nation and Bedlam Entertainment Inc., to help us develop the most exciting, educational, and engaging summit we can. We are also working with The Guru Nation to build a library of Creating WE tools, webinars, and interviews so everyone can learn more about the neuroscience of WE online: www.thegurunation.com.

Harvard Medical School: Since the writing of 42 Rules, we've made an alliance with Srini Pillay, M.D., Harvard Medical School Assistant Clinical Professor of Psychiatry and CEO, Neurobusiness Group. With the help of his expertise, we will be developing products and services to advance our ability to shape our neural networks to be more adaptable to change and to enable people to actively shift into more positive mindsets.

HeartMath: Also, we have formed an alliance with Bruce Cryer and the HeartMath Institute. Additionally, a number of our Creating WE Institute colleagues have been certified to be HeartMath One-on-One Providers. Each one of us believes in the power of the heart to create coherence, and we know from 15 years of research at the HeartMath Institute that the more we can move ourselves into coherence individually and collectively, the more we can gain clarity of thinking and health of our minds, hearts, bodies and spirits.

Liminal Group: For the past five years we've worked with Scudder Fowler and the Liminal Group to bring our keynotes to leaders around the United States. This year we've created the Actor's Studio, a series of in-depth interviews that we will be conducting with incredible leaders and neuroscientists who are changing the face of business and whose ideas we want to get out to larger audiences.

Global Platinum Group: For the past five years we've worked with a powerful diagnostic and assessment tool based on a unique and powerful platform. We have been working with this tool, and with the Global Platinum Group to create a more powerful process for leaders to understand how to collectively and accurately determine how to focus energy on customers, employees, leaders and cultural issues. The predictive nature of this tool is astounding, and its power to create alignment is in a class of its own.

Client Summits: We are continually seeking new alliances, partnerships, research opportunities and clients who want to learn more about Creating WE ideas, technologies, practices and how to accelerate successful collaboration inside and outside of their organizations. We've gotten requests to bring our summits into client organizations so people can learn together about how to be more 'human together' and can work to shape their workplaces to become innovation engines and great places to work.

However, all of this is just the beginning. We are learning to deepen our conversations and expand our interests in listening to people from all walks of life and from around the globe. There is so much to learn, and to share. We are here for the journey and welcome you aboard!

Introduction

"Where the Art of Engagement and the Spirit of Innovation Build Collective Wisdom in the Workplace."

The Creating WE Institute is an international cadre of critical thinkers, consultants, coaches and scientists with multi-disciplinary expertise, who have come together to harvest new forms of engagement and innovation in the workplace and in the world.

We believe that WE are all connected. Through a WE-centric rather than a traditional I-centric approach, our collective wisdom grows and evolves, creating stronger solutions and mutual respect for the unique contributions of others.

We-centric thinking can change the very nature of leadership, culture, brands, businesses and other organizations...and it all starts with conversation.

You are invited to explore and dialogue with The Creating We Institute. We hope you will contact us to talk about how we can engage with you and your organization, leaders and employees, to help change how conversations take place at work. Find out how the power of Creating WE is changing how leaders lead, and how it can change the tenor and context of your organizational culture, now and for years to come.

The Creating WE Institute is engaged in ongoing research, exploring the dynamics of thought leadership, and how leaders emerge, engage and evolve.

The membership of the Institute is composed of a unique amalgam of critical thinkers, consultants and other practitioners engaged in pursuits ranging from pure research to active application of the latest techniques, insights and technologies to change outcomes.

As an adjunct to our research, and on a contractual basis, The Creating WE Institute accepts engagements and provides services and products to clients who are interested in expanding their organizations' capacity for success, growth and development from I-centric to WE-centric thinking.

Our services reflect a range of collective Institute expertise at the vanguard of change. We work with clients on engagements that focus on executive, team, and organizational coaching and consulting. We utilize several products and various assessments that are customized to determine and meet our clients' emerging needs. We welcome conversations, inquiries, questions and dialogues on any and all of the themes and principles offered in '42 Rules for Creating WE.'

Section I
Shatter Old Paradigms

- Rule 1: Rules are Meant to Be Broken

- Rule 2: There Is No Quid Pro Quo in WE

- Rule 3: Be Selfish to Become Selfless

- Rule 4: Live in Your Heart's Zone

1 Rules are Meant to Be Broken

Michelle Boos-Stone

To create WE, we can't simply focus on our existing rules and demand others follow them.

Most of us have been brought up by rules: The Golden Rule, The Ten Commandments, and general 'Rules to Live By.' Rules are such an ingrained part of our culture and our everyday thinking that they have become almost invisible to our very own eyes.

Some rules are created for the betterment of mankind, and give us a shared framework for success: "Treat others as you would want them to treat you," and "Share what you have with others." Other rules are made to create compliance to strict guidelines; such as the laws our countries are governed by, which ultimately are intended to avoid chaos and anarchy.

Rules exist in every aspect of our lives, whether they are assumed, written, or made up, and every day we live our lives by these rules. Yet sometimes, when we feel so strongly about our own rules they can *bind* us to fight for our views, and *blind* us to the views of others.

Some rules are *meant* to be broken, especially when it comes to Creating WE—so we will explore new possibilities together and create rules we both embrace with passion and enthusiasm.

To create a true sense of WE it's important for us to:

- Commit to thinking differently about rules!
- Create and nurture environments that foster rule *breaking*, not just rule following.

- Give people permission to take risks and make mistakes.
- Foster 'possibility thinking' over 'rule following.'
- Be willing to let go of (or re-examine) rules we've self-created.

The rules we 'make up' are often the ones meant to be broken. To grow ourselves and others, consider shifting from demanding rules to exploring *possibilities*. Possibilities allow us to stretch our own thinking and incorporate others' best ideas in unimaginable new ways. They encourage us to ask deeper questions that lead us to deeper shared insights and wisdom.

Possibility thinking asks us to imagine:

- What haven't we thought of yet?
- How thinking differently allows us to create something better and different?
- If we shift the way we do this, could our approach be game-changing?
- What happens if we/I don't change and things stay the same?
- Which key stakeholders have a vested interest in things being different?
- What could the future look like if we could have it exactly as we wanted it?

We can't get to WE when we are only focused on the rules that must be followed. Instead we must focus on **what could be** and harness our collective intelligence by breaking old mental models and to think...and act differently to create outrageous possibilities!

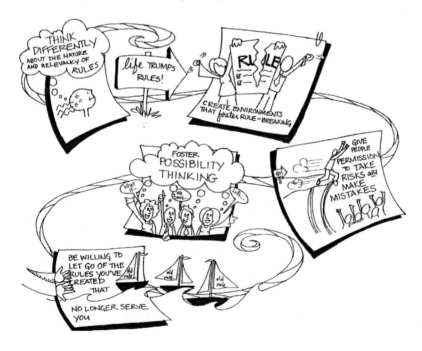

2

There Is No Quid Pro Quo in WE

Bud Bilanich

Too many people wait for others to go first.

WE is built on relationships; the idea that we are all connected, and that through a WE-centric, rather than a traditional I-centric approach, our collective wisdom grows and evolves. This kind of thinking creates stronger organizations and societies. It fosters mutual respect for the unique contribution every person is capable of making. Solid, lasting, mutually-beneficial relationships are at the core of WE. Giving with no expectation of return is a great way to create these types of relationships.

However, we live in a quid pro quo world: you do for me and I'll do for you. While there is nothing wrong in reciprocating a good deed or a favor, there is a fundamental problem with quid pro quo. It is reactive not proactive. Too many people wait for others to go first. They adopt the attitude, "When and if you do for me, I'll do for you." This scarcity mentality is not conducive to creating WE. When you come from a scarcity mentality, you focus on holding on to what you already have; this can prevent you from receiving what you might possibly get.

On the other hand, giving with no expectation of return comes from a proactive abundance mentality. When you give with no expectation of return, you are acknowledging the abundance of the universe. You are demonstrating faith that the good you do will benefit others close to you and the world at large—and that good things will come back to you.

Giving with no expectation of return is ironic. I have found that the more I give, the more I receive, and often from unlikely sources. But that's not my reason for giving—and I hope it is not yours. The best reason for giving is the basic joy of making a difference in other people's lives and in creating a WE-centric world.

I love the Liberty Mutual Insurance 'responsibility' ads. They are a very visual demonstration of the ideas behind creating WE—especially giving with no expectation of return. You've probably seen them. They begin with someone going a little out of their way to do something that benefits others; picking up a piece of trash, or opening a door for another person whose hands are full. Another person observes this and goes out of their way for someone else. The cycle repeats several times during the ad. The message is clear. We are all better off when we help each other.

Giving without expectation of return not only helps you create a WE-centric culture, it helps you build strong partnerships. Life and Success Coach Larry Agresto is a WE-centric guy. He says, "Truly successful people never compete, they network and leverage their relationships by providing value and giving more than they receive."

In the end, giving with no expectation of return comes down to your mentality—scarcity or abundance. If you come from a scarcity mentality, you will live by quid pro quo, and perpetuate the I-centric status quo. If you come from an abundance mentality, you will give with no expectation of return and begin to create a WE-centric world.

I choose abundance and to take an active part in creating a WE-centric paradigm in my circle of influence. I agree with Winston Churchill who once said, "We make a living by what we get, we make a life by what we give." When you give with no expectation of return you will get a good life. You'll also get a better world; one in which we all look out for one another.

3

Be Selfish to Become Selfless

Nancy Ring

Selfless leaders build a strong WE by first being selfish enough to ensure they are an effective I.

Selfish. There are few things we could say about a leader that would be more damning. Yet without being selfish enough to do what we need to be effective, we cannot become selfless.

Like it or not, we all have needs and become stressed when they are not met. This reactive stress behavior renders us ineffective, thereby undermining the power of WE.

Let's take the leadership team of XYZ Technologies, for example. Six of its leaders would fly in from all over the US and Europe to their monthly team meetings right outside of London. Because their time and travel were expensive, they packed in as much work as possible into two days.

They worked through lunch, and often through dinner as well. Then it was a 9:00 nightcap in the hotel's bar, a few hours of email, and maybe four hours of sleep before starting the next day. Yet despite all this focus on activity, they never seemed to get enough done. "How is it that the more we do, the more there is to do? If we delegate one more thing our next level managers will revolt!"

So focused on being selfless, this team was not getting its needs met. Sitting on planes and in meetings ignored their high need to be physically active. Their stress reaction was to create unnecessary activity and busy-ness for themselves and others—effectively undermining their ability to actually accomplish their goals.

The solution? The team took a chance and became 'selfish.' They shortened their meeting times, and structured breaks into their agenda so everyone could leave the room and go for a walk. In addition, they made sure the team members had an opportunity to move around the meeting room rather than staying seated all day. As an added bonus, they also committed to exercising before or after work.

By productively channeling their physical energy into exercise, the team was able to think more clearly, and to organize their activities together. In a clearer state of mind, they stopped making up additional projects for themselves and others that did not add value. They realized that by doing less, they accomplished more—all made possible by being selfish—that is, they took the time to recognize and attend to their own needs.

How about you?

Do you know what you need to be effective in your life? Do you know how much time and information you need to make sound decisions and build that into your work plan? Or, do you force yourself to decide quickly without all the data you need, stress out, and make more work for everyone by changing the decision, or forcing the ineffective decision to work?

Perhaps you find that too many meetings with too many people leave you cranky and impatient? By 'selfishly' scheduling enough time every day to recharge on your own, you could be more a selfless meeting participant, one who is better able to participate in the process rather than obstruct it.

Being selflessly selfish can go even further. Have you found that you are better able to be objective and focus on the facts after you've had a chance to express your feelings? If so, be selfish. Find a trusted colleague who can listen empathetically and help you clear emotions that may cloud your thinking.

Selfish leaders—those who pay attention to their own needs—enable others to do the same. Once we take care of our own needs, we become more open to listen and pay attention to others—we become selfless. Selfless leaders have learned to recognize when their responses are reactions to stress and which unmet needs are the cause. In these situations, they know what measures to take to have these needs met and ensure they are quickly acted upon so they can return to working effectively with others.

Selfless leaders build a strong WE by first being selfish enough to ensure they are an effective I.

4

Live in Your Heart's Zone

Bruce Cryer, Judith E.
Glaser, and Nancy Ring

Actually, it took recognizing my own judgments and emotions as the true source of my stress that changed—even saved—my life.

Negative emotions can play a powerful role in our relationships with others. It's possible to rewire our mental, emotional and physical reactions—you just need to know how.

Now, several years down the line, Jack looks back on his experience with Tom and realizes that it changed his life—for the better.

Tom and Jack, both part of Chemco's decentralized IT function, lobbied hard to gather their colleagues into a single department. After the CEO appointed them co-leaders of the new group, word was out on the street: "Doomed to fail. These guys are like oil and water!"

"And they were right," remembers Jack. Tom was known for his laser-like intellect, his warm wit, and a temper that cut people off at their knees.

"Everyone thought I was the cool, detached, calm one," Jack continues. "Little did they know I was seething beneath the veneer. Tom's unpredictable moods left me exhausted and I was convinced his explosions would bring us down. Actually, it took recognizing my own judgments and emotions as the true source of my stress that changed—even saved—my life."

How did Jack come to such a major revelation? He literally had a change of heart.

HeartMath's eighteen years of scientific research have shown that our hearts have the ability to calm our fight-or-flight reactions to stress, thereby allowing our brains, hearts, and bodily functions to synchronize naturally. Once Jack began using HeartMath's simple five-step process of detaching, breathing in a ten-second rhythm, connecting to positive feelings, opening to new possibilities, and anchoring his new perspectives, he began rewiring his mental, emotional, and physical reactions to Tom—and to all the potential stressors in his life.

Here's how one of the HeartMath® key techniques works:

First, take a break—even momentarily—and detach yourself from the situation. Their research shows that freezing and disengaging from our emotional reactions interrupts the process whereby the brain's amygdala connects the current experience to memories of similar events, and triggers a series of 1,400 biochemical reactions that stimulate our fight-or-flight response. Interrupting this process saves us from a rush of the stress hormone cortisol, which has been linked to a long list of maladies including sleeplessness, ulcers, and heart disease.

Second, focus your attention on the area around your heart. Imagine breathing through your heart: inhale to the count of five, and exhale for another five seconds. This simple breathing technique brings the heart—your most powerful organ—into sync (or coherence) with the rest of your body. Coherence then triggers feelings of well-being in the brain, which can accurately be sent to the rest of your system to alleviate anxiety and other negative reactions.

The *third* step is to connect with positive feelings by recalling experiences that easily and reliably make you feel good. Fanning those sincere feelings enables your amygdala to match your current experience with a positive emotional response, thereby opening your brain to creative, innovative, and helpful ways to handle what's before you.

Fourth, ask yourself (and perhaps others involved) what other perspectives or approaches would alleviate stress now, and in the future. Now that stress is no longer blocking your own creativity and internal wisdom, you will be amazed at the brighter possibilities that appear. This stress-free objectivity enables you to see the wisdom in others' ideas as well.

Fifth, spend some time—as much as possible—reflecting on the shifts you've made and anchoring them into new ways of thinking, feeling, and acting. This will enable you to expand your learning beyond your current experience.

"It's this last step that enabled me to reap lessons from reframing my reactions to Tom and translate them into other circumstances and relationships," Jack reports. "I would never have been able to take on HR and Finance without these techniques," he adds.

Like many other successful leaders, Jack experienced how changing our approach to stress can change our lives.

Section II
Acknowledge the 'I' Inside the 'WE'

- Rule 5: There is an 'I' in Team
- Rule 6: Speak from the 'I'—Listen from the 'WE'
- Rule 7: Become a Creating WE Leader
- Rule 8: Seek to Mine for Value
- Rule 9: Take Your Seat at the Table and Use It!

5 There is an 'I' in Team

Jerry Manas

The 'I's' in the team were now allowed to shine in their own terms, which resulted in a kinder work environment, a more productive staff, more satisfied customers and a true WE spirit.

In an effort to create a WE atmosphere, some leaders try to have everyone move together as if they're in a chain gang, all clones of one another moving in the same direction. Instead, we must celebrate the diversity on our teams, and leverage the different strengths people have. There's a time for individual achievement and a time for convergence as a team. We need to give equal attention to both.

I was called into one organization to help them create a process and structure for a department that supported and maintained financial systems. "We're having problems with one person in particular," the director, Patty, told me. "Max just seems to march to his own agenda. He's great at what he does, and is probably our best person, but he's not good at communicating with our clients." "How can we turn him around?" she asked.

My immediate reaction was, "Why on earth would you want to turn him around if he's your best employee?" It was apparent that they had spent quite a bit of time trying to turn Max into a 'customer service rep' instead of the technician that he was and a brilliant one at that.

They were frustrated and so was he. I was reminded of the Robert Heinlein quote: *Never try to teach a pig to sing. It wastes your time and annoys the pig.*

This is exactly what they were trying to do—teach the pig to sing. I suggested that they stop wasting energy trying to 'turn around' Max, but that they should instead let Max do what he does best, and pair him with someone who excels at customer service. It just so happened that there was someone else in the department who was *extremely* customer-oriented, and could fit quite well as a liaison between Max and the customers. When Patty suggested that this person may not have time, I was able to find several things on that person's plate that were much better suited for someone else in the group.

Management wrote off another person on the team as a slacker, and as it turned out, this person wasn't a slacker at all. He was just apathetic because he wasn't engaged and wasn't operating in his area of strength. He was an analyst, who preferred heads-down detailed logical work. Yet he was being asked to facilitate and lead projects—a bad fit if I ever saw one. As soon as he was given the proper support and appropriate work for his strengths, he grew less apathetic and at least gave a good day's effort.

One by one, we assessed where people were playing to their strengths, and where they weren't. After a few weeks of getting a feel for people's strengths, adjusting their roles accordingly, and involving them in creating processes that helped instead of hindered, the department began to operate much more cohesively.

When I first arrived, the client complained about having too many 'heroes,' dysfunction among the team, and just plain poor performers. The client felt they lacked the ingredients to become a WE-centric team. Yet these so-called barriers were just symptoms—a mirage hiding the real problem. This is often the case when people are misaligned or not allowed to let their individuality shine.

There's much talk about the danger of 'heroes,' yet great achievements have often been a result of heroic efforts on the part of a few people, and sometimes even one person. It's one of the world's biggest myths about teamwork that there's no 'I' in Team. In fact there *is* an 'I' in Team; there are many 'I's, each with their own strengths and preferences. And the faster we recognize that, the faster we'll succeed at creating WE.

In the case of my client, the 'I's' in the team were now allowed to shine in their own terms, which resulted in a kinder work environment, a more productive staff, more satisfied customers and a true WE spirit.

6

Speak from the 'I'—Listen from the 'WE'

Judith E. Glaser

Difficult conversations are challenging, yet when one 'I' meets another 'I' in candor and caring, they form a perfect WE.

Difficult conversations and disagreements can be challenging. When we are at odds with others we often feel competitive, as though we are in a win/lose situation. Being on opposite sides of an issue with someone can lead us to feel like we are in conflict with them, which can cause us to feel like we are foes and not friends.

Once we label someone a foe, we tend to treat them as a foe, and often fall into patterns of behavior that continuously push them away. By changing a label from foe to friend, we activate a whole new set of patterns of interaction that move us toward rather than away from them. The way to move someone from foe to friend is to speak from the 'I' and listen from the 'WE.'

I implemented this strategy a few years ago when I was introduced to a new colleague. When we met we immediately hit it off. We had similar business interests, which seemed to pull us toward each other. Consequently, we decided to work on projects together and attempt to form a partnership.

We developed ideas and created plans to go after business together. I introduced her to many of my clients and she introduced me to some of hers. Both of us put a lot of energy into the process, so much so that we were redirecting energy away from our own individual work, onto this new 'dream' we both shared of creating something bigger than each of us could do alone.

I found myself starting to keep track and score of 'my giving and my getting back.' Part me of knew this wasn't a healthy practice, but at the time, I was grasping for a more concrete understanding of how our partnership was playing out. Once I realized I was the 'time investor with no return,' I got angry and did something that was neither helpful for her or me—I kept my feelings to myself.

Instead of airing my frustration and issues by speaking from the 'I' and listening from the 'WE,' I simply pretended that everything was okay. In the meantime, I was ranting and complaining to everyone else. I was afraid to confront my colleague out of the fear that doing so would ruin our friendship. Without even being aware of it, my misdirected complaints transformed me into the enemy.

I eventually decided to call up my colleague and ask her for some time for us to talk. Rather than project my anger on her, I decided to share my emotions in a new way: by speaking from the 'I' and listening from the 'WE.'

"I have been upset over our business partnership. I started to keep score on how much time I invested, and felt I was the giver and you were not. I didn't share this with you out of fear that it would ruin our relationship, but the more time I invested the angrier I got. We have a great dream and I want to work out our rules of agreement so we can continue to create something bigger than either of us could create alone."

From this new perspective, I realized that:

- By keeping score and not making my feelings transparent, I had made both of us enemies.
- Releasing emotions that were getting in the way of Creating WE, enabled a new friendship to emerge.
- When speaking to someone with whom you need to 'work out issues,' speak from your authentic 'I.'
- One should share feelings in a candid, not judgmental, way.
- It is important to be caring and open but not blameful.

Difficult conversations are challenging, yet when one 'I' meets another 'I' in candor and caring, they form a perfect WE. When we are able to step into each other's shoes and appreciate the world from each other's perspective—seeking to connect—everything changes.

7

Become a Creating WE Leader

Cindy Tortorici

Maximize the *individual*, create a community of *people*, and define the *purpose*.

If we look back to the beginning of time, we see the same human needs emerge over and over again: to be effective, leaders need to know themselves—what's energizing, and what's draining, and they need to know what turns others on and off as well. Most importantly, they need to know how to awaken this wisdom in themselves and others. Without self-awareness, leaders cannot lead.

Becoming a WE-centric leader is not something we do overnight. For many of us, it's a lifelong quest. Yet all too often, we shortchange the journey and define leadership as 'a process and/or a tactical application of principles.' When you 'Google' the term 'leadership,' you'll find charts, lists, and complex theories that promise to 'transform' the team, and allow it to 'soar' to a higher level.

You'll also find websites designed to help leaders manage the performance review process or performance problems, protecting the organization from litigation and human resource issues. And while these objectives all have their place, they are not the basis of true leadership.

In our challenging and unpredictable global environment, the truth is that we are viscerally most attracted to leaders who are self-reflective about their leadership, and who inspire this same reflection in others.

When we look back at leadership with the lens of cutting-edge sustainability, we see that the best of the best focus not on the processes and the tactics, but on helping people bring their whole person to work. Through this process of self-exploration, they learn how to maximize the greatness each person brings to their life and their job.

WE-centric Leadership... The Essential and Vital Three

The big question, of course, is how do you take on something that is defined so clearly and simply, yet is obviously quite difficult to achieve? When one of the key elements in that definition is out of alignment, the leader is less effective. Here are the three most important insights that leaders need to focus on, in order to be WE-centric leaders.

Maximize the *Individual*

Leadership originates with the individual. The most successful businesses recognize that every person in the company can be a leader. The most sustainable practices today focus on how each person's unique capabilities combine with their passions and values. The best practices ask the question, "What is each individual's 'pattern of success' that influences (leads) the team to achieve the shared purpose or vision?" Clarifying and celebrating that contribution is a vital step in developing great leaders who can reliably achieve sustainable success.

Create a Community of *People*

Latest neuroscience research demonstrates that human beings are social beings. More than anything we need and want to be connected to others. We seek meaningful connections with others; we crave belonging and inclusion. Being rejected is as painful—some say more painful—than death. Yet, even when surrounded by people all day, many of us feel cut off from the community. Why? Beyond simple interactions with others, we want strong, human relationships with those whose ideas, actions and vision match ours or oppose ours in a stimulating and constructive way.

Define the *Purpose*

Leadership today—and, one could argue, every day—is about establishing trust, internally and externally around a common purpose. This process begins at the highest levels in our world and flows into our organizations and our relationships. Then purpose flows through each individual into the team and moves outward to envelop our clients with quiet authority. Creating a shared purpose is essential and vital to every organization's success.

WE-centric leadership in twelve words or less: Maximize the *individual*, create a community of *people*, and define the *purpose*. Simple yet so powerful!

8 Seek to Mine for Value

Dale Kramer Cohen

When we seek to mine for value, we endow meaning to members beyond merely their function, and we inspire them to contribute their full potential

When we enter a meeting room filled with colleagues we often think about how we will be perceived. Will Joe in the corner think I'm smart enough? Will Debra dismiss my ideas again? Will Bill assume he knows my opinion and interrupt?

What if, instead, we thought about the value Joe, Debra, and Bill could each bring to the project and then collaborated to achieve our goals?

In today's 24/7/365 world, we barely have a minute to think, let alone reflect. Meetings convene, agendas are presented and we jump in. While we know we have to consider each person's role, do we really make the time? Or is this the area we shortchange without even realizing it, and then watch the precipitous decline in the organic growth of these critical relationships?

To ensure each individual's value and strength is accessed, and optimized, the WE-centric leader must continuously strive to mine the gifts and potential contributions of each team member.

Take Luisa, for example, Executive Director of a non-profit organization who had a smart, eager staff dedicated to the cause. She was passionate, brilliant, and determined to see the organization flourish. She had great vision and drive. She was also efficient and officious and drove her overworked team rigidly. While she was achieving her success, her 'I'-centric approach would never bring forth the best from each team member, rather, it posed to undermine the team's future success.

How WE Engage

Imagine the benefit to the business if she took the time to recognize the fresh, fearless vantage that the new philosophy-major-analyst brought to the table or the new leadership skills that the IT Director had acquired from her volunteer Board position outside of work. In being so determined to develop the organization, Luisa had forgotten about the very people who helped built it and the talents they possessed.

Forcing her to take the time to step back and clearly 'see' the individuals in her team, and not just their titles, was the first step. Impersonal commands such as, "Oh we need IT to do this," or, "Marketing Team, you do that," needed to be modified to address individuals, like herself, who wanted to be valued and appreciated as part of the WE. That meant mapping each person and identifying their value to the team for current and future goals.

When Luisa consciously considered each person's value *before* her next big meeting, she was stunned at how such simple groundwork could reap fundamental benefits. She recognized that in order to create a WE, it is incumbent on each leader to seek and mine each team member's strengths and value and unleash them to propel the team into unparalleled terrain and success.

Some simple steps to mine for team-member value are:

- Just as you prepare for a meeting, take time to consider *who* is part of the WE.
- Make a list of each individual and what you see as their strengths and value.
- Meet with these individuals and see what *they* perceive as their strengths and value to the team.
- Map needed value and consider where each individual's value would be greatest.
- Consciously provide each team member specific opportunities to demonstrate their prowess in that area.
- Create WE and consider:
  - Did I help each person take their vast talent to contribute optimally?
  - Did I help each person climb to their best, in the meeting/within this initiative?
  - Did I leverage this person's strengths by anticipating their ability to serve the goal based on their competence, confidence, and capabilities?

Each of us wants to be valued—by our peers, our boss, our team members, and our organization. When we seek to mine for value, WE endow meaning to each member beyond merely their function, and we inspire them to contribute their full potential to the team and entire organization—this is transformational!

9

Take Your Seat at the Table and Use It!

Cindy Tortorici

Teams that Create WE depend on your perspective and experience. To Create WE, you need to make the most of your seat by contributing with confidence.

Many people take their role on the team for granted. We often don't realize that everything we do will have an impact. If we show up with only half a heart, or half our attention to the matters at hand, we will be shortchanging the team as well as ourselves.

With a bit of courage this can shift dramatically. Courage? Yes, courage. It takes courage to take your 'full' seat at the table. Why? Because we are committing to bring out our ideas, and thinking—even if others at first disagree. We may get push back or responses we may not have expected, yet this is part of the journey we will need to take to get to the top.

It can be uncomfortable to make a change in the way we contribute to the team. But the reality is, as we progress in our careers, we must evolve and grow because we are ultimately expected to contribute at a higher level to the strategic team and to achieving results. This means stepping up and into a role that has impact. This means showing up with confidence and using our experience to make a difference. It takes some practice to change the way we behave. Here are some ideas to help you take your seat and use it!

Think BIG

Most meetings are tactical in nature but have an inherent opportunity to create positive change and/or momentum. Maximize your seat by thinking BIG! Take each group to a higher level by providing an atmosphere for all to flourish. Ask BIG questions that cause people to think WE together.

For example:

- What does success look like?
- How can we describe our next greatest accomplishment as a team?
- How can we challenge each other to think bigger than we've ever thought before?

Think in a critical and strategic manner to provide vision, purpose and a roadmap to achieve your goals and the organization's goals.

Get Outside

Bring new perspective to your organization by participating outside the company in a neutral network of peers and mentors. It is easy to become absorbed in the company culture and lose perspective. Often, this may lead to a loss of confidence to test new ideas. Take risks and be sure to confront the fear of failure.

A neutral network of peers and mentors provides context on the broader worldview, which leads to offering and making better suggestions and decisions. Seek out opportunities to connect with others who will help you create mind space for innovative ideas and strategies.

For instance, join a nonprofit or for profit board, volunteer for an organization whose mission you are passionate about; take a cooking class, participate in Toastmasters. Find the time and participate! Then bring your new perspectives back to share with others inside your organization—so you expand the WE-centric thinking where you work.

Communicate with Purpose

Some people talk too much, and when they do their most important message or idea may get lost. Some people don't communicate enough and lose the opportunity to lead and influence, and worse yet, can become invisible. Both of these examples are dangerous to a WE-centric team. Be prepared for the meeting and clear on what you want to achieve before you get there so you can be sure to get your ideas heard. Think before you speak but always speak!

At any given boardroom table there are perhaps 12 seats. You must make your contribution count! Teams that Create WE depend on your perspective and experience. To Create WE, you need to make the most of your seat by contributing with confidence.

Section III
Understand What Moves People

- Rule 10: Create a Virtual Water Cooler
- Rule 11: Living the Brand Creates WE
- Rule 12: Harness Collective Wisdom
- Rule 13: Respond with "Yes!"
- Rule 14: Sometimes Thinking Small Has Big Payoffs
- Rule 15: Be Consciously Contagious

10

Create a Virtual Water Cooler

Jerry Manas

It was a new way to communicate, and much more efficient. In many cases, it negated the need for meetings.

Increasingly, organizations must adapt to people working offsite, from home, or in remote locations. What we lose with this is the 'water cooler' effect, the simple camaraderie and information sharing which happens at the water cooler, found in a shared common area. To remedy this, it's important to understand how tools such as social networks, blogs, and virtual worlds can be leveraged to minimize these gaps. Properly used, these tools can boost a feeling of teamwork and raise productivity.

Let's take Bob for example. Bob works from home most of the time as a software developer. He is one of his company's most productive and valued employees, doing most of his work in the comfort of his own home, without the commute time and the interruptions typical of most workplaces. Yet when he first started working from home, he saw there was also a downside to it. He felt 'out of touch' and disconnected from other people. He had trouble reaching people on the phone if he needed to, whether it was waiting to hear from a customer for feedback on a prototype, or needing to hear from another technical person in order to complete a certain function. He also missed the idle chat that he used to have in the office to add levity to the day.

Then some of his colleagues began talking about social media tools, such as Twitter, Facebook, Blogs and Wikis. To start with, he set up a Facebook profile, and joined a Facebook group that many of his teammates were members of.

The group was set up specifically for Information Technology people in his company. To his surprise, he noticed from their profiles that a number of his colleagues shared many of his interests not only work-related, but music, books, movies, and sports as well.

And, by way of their status updates, he was able to see what they were up to during the course of the day. He would comment occasionally on their updates, and they would comment on his. In a funny sort of way, he began to feel more connected to them. All of a sudden, these colleagues, some halfway across the world, became his friends. He began feeling more comfortable asking them questions, and his relationship with them became more collaborative.

Then, Bob began experimenting with other tools. He subscribed to one colleague's blog to stay in touch with what the latest trends were in that person's area of expertise. And he found that by using Twitter he could exchange brief messages about specific projects with any number of people in the company, including clients, teammates, and managers. Anyone who wanted to be 'in the know' on the project would simply subscribe to the appropriate feed, getting updates via email or directly to their cell phones if they chose. And anyone on the team could contribute to the feed as well. It was a new way to communicate, and much more efficient. In many cases, it negated the need for meetings.

All too often in companies, we don't find time to communicate, even when we are co-located. Relationships tend to be built more in hallways, in the lunchroom, or at the water cooler. Whether we're co-located or working virtually, we can boost this water cooler effect by creating online spaces for people to build relationships and communicate. Some organizations fear that people will abuse this, and spend all their time gossiping. Those who have leveraged these tools know better. They know that the benefits far outweigh the risks.

Creating WE is all about communication. And social media tools can boost communication to an unprecedented level, what we can call our CQ or 'Communication Quotient.' This means work-related communication and relationship building, which is equally important for true, lasting productivity.

11

Living the Brand Creates WE

Brian Penry

Focus on creating WE around the most powerful feature of your organization: one that truly exemplifies your brand—while differentiating and distinguishing it among all others.

Mission or value statements are intended to instill shared sets of beliefs throughout an organizational culture, yet they are often ignored. While this is due to several reasons, it is often because they lack relevance or passion.

Our authentic sense of self, and in turn, our sense of 'WE,' generates from being part of, and giving to something bigger—rather than from following the seemingly arbitrary guidelines and intentions of official statements. Here is a unique, simple, and highly effective approach to creating a culture of WE. By setting a brand identity-driven common goal throughout all levels of your organization, you can achieve success that is anything but 'common.'

Focus on creating WE around the singular, most powerful feature of your business or organization: the one that truly exemplifies your brand identity. In the process, you may find, as some of the following brands have and their outstanding successes attest, that brand identities can be incredibly effective vehicles, not only for engaging people throughout your organization, but for sparking their individual passion as well.

Rather than the obvious aspects of your brand identity (ID), such as its logo, etc., our focus is instead on its essence: that one, outstanding feature with which it is most readily associated—and which differentiates and distinguishes your brand ID among all others.

For example, the central feature of Southwest Airlines' brand ID is being the low-cost airline. For Disney, it is creating happiness for people of all ages, everywhere. For Apple and its brand family of 'i' products, it is being a leading technology innovator. By associating such simple, overarching themes with their brand identities, these and other organizations help drive decisions throughout all levels of their enterprise, in ways more powerful than any mission or value statement ever could. The formula is simple:

Brand Identity + 1 Compelling Feature =
An Ideal Driver for Creating a Culture of WE

When associated with your most compelling feature, your brand ID can be the ultimate driver of behaviors within your organization—in turn, driving its culture and success.

Belonging, Influencing and Reflecting Our Essence: A brand ID-driven culture of WE not only gives each individual in your organization a powerful sense of belonging and purpose beyond their job description, it gives them direct influence on your brand identity—a positive, if not cathartic, process.

From acting in the belief that they are making a real difference (and they are) to ideating ways of improving performance, even using the most informal settings as opportunities—everything your people do or say reflects on your brand. It always did, of course. However, given this context, the words and actions of every member of your organization can have an even more profound influence on how others perceive it.

Case in Point: In addition to the potential of a brand ID-driven culture of WE within your organization, consider the even greater, external possibilities, as exemplified by Skype—best known for free, peer-to-peer, Internet telecommunications.

With earnings of only $11 million, Skype's $2.6 billion sale to eBay was driven by something much greater than its earnings potential: its customers. Representing even greater promise by almost doubling since the sale, this external, brand ID-driven culture of WE is now almost 100 million strong.

Yet, its impressive growth still isn't why it was, and continues to be, so highly valued: it is because its members are advocates. They not only continually prove their worth by telling others about Skype brand products and services; they represent the ability to do even more for additional brands. Most importantly, they do it through the Internet—the fastest growing multiplier of brand ID-driven cultures of WE.

Harness Collective Wisdom

Jerry Manas

There seems to be some unspoken "don't ask, don't tell" mentality when it comes to people's backgrounds. This is a shame, because we're missing tremendous opportunities to harness collective wisdom.

How well do you know the people on your team? Does one person seem chatty while another seems aloof? Does one drive hard to "just get it done" while another wants to examine all the variables first? Does one seem overly sensitive while another seems cold and methodical? Does anyone seem resentful that they're not being consulted more? Finally, have you thought about why these people act that way, or better yet how to leverage these differences?

A team is made up of individuals, and each person brings to the table their personal wisdom including their cultural upbringing, their ethnicity, their genetic code, their social experiences, their home experiences, their past work experiences, and even their age and gender. These variables work collectively to make each of us unique. Which factors take priority is anyone's guess. We are like snowflakes; no two alike. People also bring a whole repertoire of knowledge and skills, many of which are never even revealed or leveraged. There seems to be some unspoken "don't ask, don't tell" mentality when it comes to people's backgrounds. This is a shame, because we're missing tremendous opportunities to harness collective wisdom.

While we must be careful about stereotyping, the more we can learn about the cultures involved on our team, the age or gender-influenced possibilities, and each individual's background and preferences, the better we'll understand and be able to leverage the people that make up our team. Equipped with this knowledge, we can assemble powerful combinations for sub-teams, make better staffing decisions, and circumvent negative conflict.

There are numerous studies highlighting the differences among cultures. For instance, Latin cultures tend to be more community and relationship-driven, while the U.S., England, and Germany tend to be more rule-oriented and goal-focused. Regarding gender, brain studies seem to support the theory that women tend to think more systematically and relationship-oriented, while men tend to think more systematically and goal-oriented.

Of course, with any of these, there are always exceptions, so it's prudent to use any generalization as a starting point (as opposed to stereotyping, which draws conclusions as an *ending point*). In other words it's a possibility that certain actions or habits could be gender or culture related, and we'd be shortsighted to not consider this at all.

To avoid any possibility of stereotyping or labeling, the Disney Institute, the training arm of The Walt Disney Company, suggests assessing people as to whether they are *relationships-driven*, *results-driven*, or both (in which case they can adapt to either role as needed). The lesson is that a team must be comprised of both roles in some combination and at different times in order to be successful. Neither role is considered 'wrong.'

As for harnessing the knowledge on our team, I've seen some organizations implement 'resume-sharing' sessions, so that teammates can get to know each other and build respect for each other's backgrounds. This also allows people to better tap one another's knowledge and skills. All too often, people are underutilized in organizations simply because nobody took the time to learn about their backgrounds, or worse prematurely labeled them.

Instead of labeling people, or judging them based solely on what we perceive, we need to take the time to dig deeper to get to know their backgrounds and their influences. We just might find that the 'baggage' they bring contains gold. In essence, by understanding and better leveraging the 'I's, we exponentially increase the value of WE.

13 Respond with "Yes!"

Louise van Rhyn

This simple improvisation exercise reminds us of the value of accepting and building on offers, rather than blocking them.

As human beings, we are tuned in to how people respond. When I am with my colleagues, I cannot stop myself from being acutely aware of how they respond to what I say and do. When others respond positively to my suggestions, I am energized. When they respond dismissively, I am drained.

When learning the skill of improvisational acting, participants play a game called "Yes, and..." In this game, people tell a story in pairs. The two people tell the story sentence by sentence. Each person responds to the other person's sentence. Each accepts what has been given to them, and builds on this idea. In this game you say, "Yes" to whatever is offered to you. If your partner starts the story by saying, *Let's go to Paris,* you start your response with *Yes, and....*

When playing this game, I am always struck by the energy and creativity that emerges when people share this experience of acceptance. However, I have also noticed how difficult it seems to be to say *Yes, and...* and not "no" or "yes-but." "No" and "Yes-but" block the story and the other person's contribution.

A while ago, I asked my colleague Sheila to play:

Me: "Let's go to Paris."
Sheila: "Yes, and we could go up the Eiffel Tower."
Me: "Yes, and we can buy a bottle of champagne at the top."
Sheila: "No, that would be too expensive!"

Even though this was a game and we were telling a story, Sheila still found it impossible to accept my suggestion. Many years of schooling in being cautious and careful had made it second nature for Sheila to respond with "No" rather than "Yes."

When partners accept each other's offers and continue to build on them, the energy is palpable. They can't stop themselves from laughing out loud as their story takes on a life of its own.

This simple improvisation exercise reminds us of the value of accepting and building on offers, rather than blocking them. A "Yes" lifts our spirits and enables us to go on, to take chances, to be bold and courageous. It inspires, energizes, invites collaboration and instills trust. "No" or "Yes-but" sucks the air out of the scene and leaves us with nowhere to go.

While "No" is a small two letter word, its meaning and impact is gigantic. We don't just hear "No." We hear "No, that was a stupid idea" or "No, you are not good enough" or "No, what idiot would think that would work?" A "No" or "Yes-but" shuts down the chances for new possibilities, diminishes the quest for risk-taking, and locks people into a mindset of limitations.

In my experience, people say "No" or "Yes-but" because they are afraid of where a "Yes" may lead. Saying "Yes" brings unpredictability. It is difficult to control an interaction where "Yes" becomes the default response (as those who have played "Yes, and..." games will testify). Saying "Yes" requires courage and a willingness to let go of notions of control.

A "Yes" is inextricably linked with a sense of possibility. Benjamin Zander, conductor of the Boston Philharmonic Orchestra and co-author of the book 'The Art of Possibility,' points out that "human beings have shining eyes in the presence of possibility—it is a psychological fact."

"Yes" responses from our colleagues enable us to think more creatively and be more innovative. In groups where people consciously choose an appreciative orientation, members report, "I feel safe and supported and this enables me to be more creative in my thinking."

Responding with "Yes" gives a message of value and recognition to the person who was courageous enough to offer a suggestion. Each "Yes" contains within it many subtle meta-messages of acceptance, value, and a willingness to go on together, to reach the stars.

Try this: Respond with "Yes" and notice the shining eyes of the people around you!

14

Sometimes Thinking
Small Has Big Payoffs

Jerry Manas

Once we decided to break the overall team into sub-teams, and then, where the sub-teams were too big, break *them* into sub-teams, our momentum and our morale increased.

When trying to achieve major initiatives with large groups of people, we often run into one of three problems and sometimes all three. First, there's often an accountability problem. It's the old adage, "If everyone is accountable, nobody is accountable." So things just don't get done. Second, we descend into analysis paralysis as teams attempt to reach consensus. Then decisions get delayed for extended periods and momentum is lost. The third side effect of large teams is that we lose engagement, as some people feel less involved than others. It's hard to involve everyone in a large team so a lot of people become disengaged, or worse, angry. That's no way to create a WE-centric environment.

Many successful organizations address these issues by breaking teams into small sub-teams. Having small teams promotes distributed accountability, results in faster decision-making, and boosts engagement. Is there a specific relationship of team size to overall performance? Is there a certain size that works best? Much depends on the nature of the work.

The general thinking is that *two* is not enough diversity and/or can lead to a stalemate. *Four* can lead to taking sides. *Three* is arguable. In one sense there's adequate diversity with three people, and it's easier to reach a majority. It's also easy to maintain frequent communication. Yet some evidence shows that there may not be enough critical mass to keep momentum going.

A number of studies have concluded that a team of five to nine people is ideal, and that large teams should be broken into sub-teams of that size. One study even concluded that *six* is the magic number. But generally, it depends on the nature of the team and its goal, and the length of the effort. I've had success with three people on many smaller efforts.

Here's an example of team size in action. I once served on the core leadership team for a 400-person, two-year, global, all-volunteer program to create two new international standards for the Project Management Institute (PMI). For the first six months, the six-person core team spent time planning the initiative and conducting preliminary research via web forums. We opened up the forums for the team-at-large to contribute their opinions on certain topics, but in general, we still hadn't thought about, or communicated, what we were going to do with the large influx of people.

We sent out a monthly notice to everyone, but that wasn't enough. The great majority of people felt like they were just "along for the ride" but not making any meaningful contribution. Worse, they felt like nothing was happening and that it was a runaway program with nobody minding the mint. The opposite was true, of course. The core team was meeting weekly and had been actively engaged but they didn't know that. Some disengaged. Some dropped out. Some began causing trouble by visibly complaining.

We knew we had to do things differently, and fast. We assembled a structure of multiple sub-teams, for editing, scheduling, quality, design, and so on. When teams were adequately staffed, we created additional roles for the rest, including 'researchers' and 'reviewers,' even breaking these groups into sub-teams. We also appointed a Communication Lead, along with a sub-team to publish a regular newsletter, with updates on team happenings and milestone status.

Once we decided to break the overall team into sub-teams, and then, where the sub-teams were too big, break *them* into sub-teams, our momentum and our morale increased. Boosting the communication helped as well. We completed the standards in record time, meeting the aggressive two-year plan when no PMI standard had ever been produced in less than three years. This was a classic example of the power of sub-teams working toward a collective whole.

When we need to create a WE spirit across a large group, we need to think in terms of small sub-teams, generally 5-9 people. This keeps people accountable, decisive, and engaged.

15

Be Consciously Contagious

Nancy Ring

If we can catch a "bad mood virus," we can transmit one too. Or, we can radiate a "great mood virus." The choice is ours.

How many times have you had this experience? You're about to sit down, and know immediately—without even looking at them—that you do not want to engage with the person next to you. Maybe you're on a plane, riding the subway, or about to eat in a crowded restaurant—and suddenly you're just certain that conversing with this person would not be a positive experience. How do you know that? How do you know that a perfect stranger is in a lousy mood before you even meet them?

Quantum physicists tell us that we humans are in constant communication with the rest of the universe. We all are radiators and receptors of energy—energy which we receive information about the world around us. Our bodies are continuously reading this information—whether we know it consciously or not. Physicists have also discovered that this energy can be felt from as far away as ten feet.

That stranger is radiating energy, which our body receives and translates into information that we factor into our decision to strike up a conversation, or in this case, to avoid it. Maybe we even change our seat—for we intuitively know that if we are not careful, we might catch that stranger's bad mood as if it were a virus. Neuroscientists have confirmed this intuition with studies that show that the more open we are to the energy of others, the more likely we are to catch their virus-like moods.

If we can catch a "bad mood virus," we can transmit one too. Or, we can radiate a "great mood virus." The choice is ours.

Starting to think a bit differently about emotions by chance? For at this point we realize that being in a good mood is not merely selfish, it is also a public service. Would your current mood help or hinder your team's progress in your 11:00 meeting? Would you want to sit next to yourself on the bus?

With just a few conscious practices we all can become radiators of good vibes at home, at work, and everywhere we go. To become an emotional public servant:

Monitor your emotions on a regular basis during the day.

Feel whatever emotions are present for you right now without any judgment whatsoever, and label them. Joy, peace, anger—just label your emotions without judging or feeding them. Then ask yourself whether your current vibe is serving you in some positive way. If so, proceed no further.

Release emotions that no longer serve you.

Once you've felt emotions that aren't serving you, you can release them using the following technique. First realize that when you judge your own emotions, or make them bigger than life, the harder they are to release. Simply hold the intention to release—or let go of the emotion while you take a few deep breaths, allowing each exhalation to wash the emotion away. Feel around the inside of the palm of your hand to find the acupressure point that also can help you release, and hold it gently. For most of us, it's in our dominant hand. Practice this in easier situations first then move to harder ones, like when you giving a speech or in the midst of a difficult conversation.

Raise your vibe so you are someone you'd want to be around.

Once you're in that neutral emotional space, raising your vibe can be as simple as thinking about something that lifts you higher and breathing into the emotion to make it bigger. Soon you're feeling it across your entire chest, and then your entire body. At that point, simply envision yourself radiating that good vibe, and enjoy.

Section IV
Foster Integrity, Candor and Caring

- Rule 16: The Torch of Integrity
- Rule 17: Tell It Like It Is
- Rule 18: Walk in Their Shoes
- Rule 19: Respect the Views of Your Adversary
- Rule 20: Forgive and Not Forget
- Rule 21: Act in a Manner That Honors Yourself and Your Associates
- Rule 22: Speak Your Vulnerable Truth
- Rule 23: Practice Presence

16 The Torch of Integrity

Deborah E. Garand

Everything we are and everything we become is from a single beacon—The Torch of Integrity.

As humans, we are undaunted seekers of truth, love, and wisdom. We are in a continuous search for how we can live this thing we call life happily and with purpose. The 'I' in us develops our realm of values—integrity provides the language. But what is integrity? What does it mean and why is it important?

Webster's Dictionary defines integrity as "soundness, an uncompromising adherence to a code of values and principles." Everything we are and everything we become is from a single beacon—the Torch of Integrity. It cannot be bought, sold or measured by any amount of money. Integrity is striving to think and act through self-respect, self-restraint, inner strength, honor and courage. It is being driven by the consideration and regard for others as well as yourself. Integrity asks you to reach higher—doing good over feeling good.

Integrity is the premise on which we build our life. We all admire, respect and seek out others who mirror our ideas of strong character. Why? Inherently, we want to trust the words, actions and intentions of one another. Integrity speaks to our ethical fiber and our sense of what is right. When we exemplify respect, virtue, honesty, excellence and many other honorable qualities within ourselves—we are building trust. Trust allows us to develop strong, honest, and authentic relationships.

Integrity challenges us to make sacrifices and to do the right thing even when doing so may prevent us from material gain or jeopardize our careers.

David, a senior executive working for a major developer, was confronted with just such a situation. He had been asked to oversee an external audit for one of their negotiated projects. Shortly into the project, the President called David into his office and passed him a letter to present to the auditors.

As David walked down the hall, he scanned the letter and realized the President was denying the existence of certain documents. David knew they existed and he knew the President knew this as well. This was David's defining moment: to risk losing his job by honoring himself and the truth, or to become complicit in the deceit. He turned around and walked back into the President's office and said, "Don, you know I am dedicated to helping you build a stronger corporation but do not ever impute my integrity. We have these records—you know it and I know it. We should always be in front of the bus—not under it."

The torch of integrity is noble, authentic and humble; the light of integrity is bright and strong, raising human spirit to its highest elevation. David spoke truth to power and by example, encouraged the President to rethink his own motivations, ethics and standards of leadership for the company.

Integrity is a 'WE-centric' expression of our highest selves. If we all strive to seek a higher elevation imagine what our world can look like! We each cast a powerful shadow that impacts every soul we meet throughout the day.

At a commencement speech, Steve Jobs from Apple Computer said, "We all die someday and facing that reality changed my life." He asks himself every morning, if he died tomorrow would he be proud of how he lived?

In the end, we will be remembered for who we are, what we stood for, how we stood for it, and whom we touched along the way.

17 Tell It Like It Is

Deborah E. Garand

Leading with trust invites trust

The best way to find out if you can trust somebody is to trust them.—Ernest Hemingway

You have heard the saying—"You may not agree with him/her but at least you know where they stand." We have probably encountered many people like this. These are individuals who aren't afraid to tell you what they think or feel. They are happy to engage in a mutual interactive dialogue that includes healthy, respectful pushback on dissenting points.

Everything is upfront. They are direct, honest and transparent, free of any pretense or deceit. They harness the power of being secure with themselves and hold themselves accountable for their thoughts and actions with a clear understanding of their values and principles. They lead with a calm inner confidence and self-trust. Leading with trust invites trust. Sounds easy, right? Wrong.

Transparency is scary for many of us, not because we are intentionally doing something wrong but because we are highly susceptible to social acceptance, judgment, criticism, and fear of retribution. To prevent us from becoming vulnerable, our brains command us to protect and defend ourselves by having a mentality of "The less they know the better."

This protective self-focus can sabotage our best intentions. We may create an atmosphere of defensiveness and build distrustful territorial silos. Instead we must have the courage to tear walls down and institute new behaviors that generate trust, cohesiveness, connectedness, and ownership. A paradigm shift toward 'WE' centric thinking expands our capacity to extend ourselves openly and honestly through the clear lens of transparency. It takes guts and courage to 'let go' of old thinking but the payoff is huge.

Ben discovered this payoff. As CEO of a highly successful sales company, Ben was positioned to double his business in 2009. Pretty good considering our economic condition! Having worked with Ben for months as his executive coach, Ben and I developed a WE-centric, transparent and comprehensive strategy. Ben was excited yet nervous. Transparency scared him. On top of this, his project managers, though loyal and hard-working, had become solo warriors and were not communicating with each other.

Ben was closing a lot of deals, running fast, overseeing every aspect of the business, but not communicating fully. Each PM knew what they were doing but felt disconnected from the whole. Protectionism, dissension, and low morale began to settle in. Ben couldn't take his company to the next level without changing his leadership and management approach.

Co-creating Conversations®

The company meeting was based upon co-creation and transparency. Leading with trust, we uncovered what was working and what was not working. The team built a structured management model to meet new demands and to hire new people. As you move through a process of co-creation with others, think about using these steps—to pave the way for success:

- Open conversations with respect for others' opinions—without making someone wrong for holding a different point of view.
- Ask 'what if' and 'help me understand your perspective' questions.
- Identify the existing situation/challenges.
- Define the goals and desired outcomes.
- Agree as a team on best practices for communicating, handling conflict, and continuing innovation conversations.
- Share and invite differing opinions—validate new ways of thinking.
- Discover and define trust, accountability, and build your culture on integrity.

By the end of the day, we had catalyzed, energized and built a powerful new team. Ben called me three weeks later and told me they were right on target and was thrilled at how productive, cohesive, and innovative his team had become.

When there is no 'perceived' hidden agenda—when what you see is what you get—there is trust. With trust there is ease, a comfort.

Leading with trust invites trust. Be transparent, speak with candor and trust yourself enough to invite others in. You will find it productive, profitable, uplifting, energizing, and a whole lot more fun!

18 Walk in Their Shoes

Deborah E. Garand

Before speaking, try to walk in their shoes.

Bringing truth and power together through understanding requires an enormous amount of courage; it is also one of the greatest attributes in 'Creating WE.'

Often, we speak and lead conversations through *our* lens and assumptions and fail to recognize or even consider other's viewpoints. Examining both perspectives affords respectful and interactive dialogue. We must therefore strive to seek understanding, and we can do this by trying to walk in the shoes of another.

Norman Schwarzkopf once said, "The truth of the matter is that you always know the right thing to do. The hard part is doing it." On one of the worst days of my professional career, I learned this statement to be truer than I ever realized.

Many years ago, I was overseeing a multi-million dollar project for a prestigious organization. A team meeting had been in session for 20 minutes as the Sr. Vice President walked in. He listened for a while and then to my horror, I watched as he began to verbally attack three of my colleagues.

As his rage escalated, tears streamed down two of the women's faces. He lambasted them for stupidity, where and how they lived and for being 'lower class.' I was in shock. I didn't know what to do or how to diffuse the situation. His rage was verbal, but its impact was physical—the women were shaking. Two of the women asked if they could leave for the day.

I was furious. This was my team and as far as I was concerned—no one deserved to be treated that way. As I was about to go into his office and "let him have it," I recognized that I needed to cool off first or risk the possibility of losing my job.

I needed to clear my head and find a way to see *beyond* his actions to understand what *drove* his actions. The only way to do this was to try and "walk in his shoes." This was no small challenge.

Knowing that abusive bullies generally try and exert control over others because of insecurity, a lack of internal strength and a need to feel powerful, I began to formulate a plan. An hour later, my best attempt for a respectful approach led with this question:

"Judd, I'm sorry to bother you. I was hoping you might *help me understand* why you responded the way you did in the meeting?"

Frustrated, he said, "It takes them forever to answer my questions, they cower and stutter and then they fumble with their paperwork."

I tried to empathize with his frustration.

Then came *my* moment of truth.

I helped Judd "walk in their shoes" so he could understand how his behavior was creating breakdowns, distrust, fear, lack of productivity and jeopardizing the deadline of the project. I was fascinated with his response. He said, "I can see the impact of my actions and will work with you on this, but the other women are weak and I don't respect weak. You are not afraid so I respect you." His response signaled important initial progress but we still had a long way to go. Self-awareness is the first, most important step to personal transformation. Without this, no change can take place.

Walking in the other person's shoes can be frightening, intimidating and daunting. We have the choice to turn a blind eye, remain quiet, mask our feelings and unknowingly, become enmeshed in living a lie or find the courage and power to connect with others deeply through *understanding their point of view*. We have the power to influence outcomes by how we choose to respond. Through exercising our ability to walk in others shoes, we move closer toward the ultimate goal of 'Creating WE.'

19 Respect the Views of Your Adversary

Whitaker Raymond and Judith E. Glaser

If we learn to refrain from trying to change others or to impose our truths on others, something positive and amazing happens.

Sometimes we end up having to work with people we just don't get along with. We are put on projects or join initiatives and we discover conflicts everywhere. Sometimes we don't even know what exactly the conflicts are all about, we just know we don't like working with the person. Other times it's really clear—we disagree about how a project is to be run, who is responsible for what, and at a deeper level, we disagree about basic values like respect, authenticity and trust.

For example, two peer managers were both asked to work in a project targeted to provide outplacement services to people about to be laid off. Both managers were assigned the task; no one had clear authority over the other. In essence both had equal voice. One manager passionately advocated for high quality outplacement services to everyone through their transition, while the other adamantly insisted on providing minimal services to only a few senior managers.

The first manager had placed strong values on the importance of respect for all employees, while the other manager valued keeping costs and financial exposure to a minimum. For many meetings they debated and argued until their boss made the decision for them.

Does this kind of adversarial situation sound familiar?

When we feel we are right, and are entrenched in our own positions, we often find fault or weakness in the other's position. Implicitly or explicitly, right or wrong, this win-lose struggle becomes a rally in which each party protects his/her own 'I.' Peppered in their language are the words, 'I', 'me', 'my', 'you' or, in instances of adversarial groups, the terms 'we', 'you' and 'they.'

The trap: In situations like these, people become adversarial—they dig in their heels and take a stand on what they believe. They adopt strong positions as a strategy to fight for their own values or beliefs. In most cases, as the exchange evolves, neither person is arguing against facts; they are, instead, trying harder to influence the other person's beliefs and values, which are often independent of facts.

The heart of the matter is that when we are entrenched in our positions we lack a genuine respect for the other person's perspective. We label the other 'side' as an enemy: wrong, bad, crazy, out of their minds, and someone to beat. We assume we are right and know the truth and we assume they are wrong so we try to persuade, convince, impose or influence the other person to yield and/or adopt our position.

The opportunity: Rather than getting pulled into battling for our positions, we can turn to thoughtful, non-reaction, non-adversarial strategies that yield tremendous value and benefit in times of conflict. Central to these strategies is a 'WE-centric' mindset in which we ac-knowledge that while we may disagree on many things, we are often similar in so many other respects.

From a WE-centric mindset—we need to seek to connect and find common ground rather than seek to make others wrong.

- **Start from common ground** – Example: First reach agreement on how quality and cost-effectiveness impact the company's health.
- **Ask questions to learn what connects you to others** – Example: "What do you see as important in coming up with a plan? Then ask more questions to learn what they are thinking... draw them out."
- **Respect the beliefs of others and seek to find out what they value and why** – Example: Highlight what the other person says is important, and then focus on what aspects you endorse and explain why.

In this spirit, we are open to recognize that our neighbors may have interests in common that we can agree upon. If we revisit our two managers who appeared on the surface to disagree on a strategy for giving outplacement to their peers, using our approach we suggest each manager ask questions to learn what is important to their ap-proach—what lies behind their positions and why they feel so strongly about them.

By doing this, we may recognize that the others' intentions, like ours, may be to create a better future, yet with a different strategy than the one we may have chosen. We discover that we both, as the greater 'WE,' may share more in common than we disagree on.

20

Forgive and Not Forget

Josephine Washington

Forgiveness practices promoted a WE-centric community built upon principles of appreciative discovery, co-creating inspiration, generative thinking and team synergy.

Too often we carry around baggage that weighs us down, causes us to hold anger toward others, and leads us to be carriers of toxic emotions. Understanding how to forgive and not forget is essential for creating WE in every organization.

Mad, hurt and confused, Steve hated his new colleague! Once again, his day at the office was miserable. Blame, blame, blame. Anger, anger, anger. Ann and Steve worked together. Steve, who worked in Sales Administration, prepared sales agreements for Ann who interfaced with customers.

Ann, the new colleague, blamed Steve for misplacing the sales agreement for the new prospective client. Sure enough, this was the same sales agreement that she took home the night before to review and did not bring back to the office, yet Steve was her target today. Frustrated by her own anger for not having the sales agreement at the office to review with the prospective client, she communicated the wrong instructions to Steve as he was preparing the new sales folder for the client.

When the client got the wrong sales agreement, he was upset and confused by the agreement details. Consequently, he decided to take his business to a competitor. Needless to say, Ann was furious at the loss of the client's business. The next day, Steve overheard Ann gossiping with the other office colleagues about how much she distrusted Steve. Steve, on the other hand, felt betrayed and wronged. Justified in his bitterness, anger, and resentment, he felt there was no apparent reason to "forgive and forget" Ann's actions.

In Steve's personal life, he had embarked on a pathway of love and forgiveness. He was healing from various personal transgressions and practiced the virtues of forgiveness daily. He started by forgiving himself, thus freeing himself of the emotional walls of bitterness, anger and resentment. He meditated in the mornings and evenings to anchor his positive thoughts for the day. Additionally, Steve mentally reflected upon situations where he practiced compassion and joy. Steve lived in his heart most of the time, practicing his mantra of "forgive and forget," except at work!

Not living in his heart at work, the place where he invested most of his emotional energies, really bothered Steve. He not only faced difficulty expressing heartfelt forgiveness, but also was equally burdened by his brain's general inability to forget the hurtful emotional situations that seemed to occur on an almost daily basis. His workplace environment, like most, was toxic and polluted with lots of negative energy, making forgetting a less than viable option. However, Steve's desire for a healthy work-life balance and for positive, WE-centric relationships propelled him to make the commitment to learn how to "forgive and *not forget*."

Immediately, Steve tried several new forgiveness practices while at work. First, he would try to envision a compassionate place for himself, a practice that allowed him to develop a greater appreciation for his own life. Second, Steve would try to view himself and his colleagues as equals and have the highest concern for enabling and ensuring their optimal performance.

Forgiveness practices promoted a WE-centric community built upon principles of appreciative discovery, co-creating inspiration, generative thinking and team synergy. Finally, Steve would try to open his heart and become more aware of the dynamics in his environment and not feel the pressure to fix everything. This practice expanded his ability to enable both his heart and mind to flow in synchrony and detect when everything is okay exactly as it is.

Finally, Steve would *not forget to give* Ann the tremendous gift of all—*his forgiveness!*

21

Act in a Manner That Honors Yourself and Your Associates

Bud Bilanich

Your actions reflect not only on you personally, but also on the groups with which you are associated.

Originally, my message here was, "Never do anything to embarrass yourself or your associates." Nancy Ring, a colleague in The Creating We Institute, pointed out that this is a negative statement; it told you what not to do. Nancy suggested that I change it to a positive statement that tells you what you should do to be a responsible member of an organization or community.

Nancy is right. It's much better to provide others with positive, affirmative actions they can use as guides for action than with negative actions to avoid. Thanks to Nancy for this bonus advice.

WE-centric thinking holds that we are all part of something bigger than ourselves. This being the case, your actions reflect not only on you personally, but also on the groups with which you are associated.

When I was in junior high school I was caught shoplifting an item that cost less than a dollar from a local discount store. I did it on a dare. My parents were obviously very upset with me because they had raised me not to lie, cheat and steal. With this little shoplifting escapade, I dishonored our family. It didn't matter that it was on a childhood dare or that "everyone else was doing it." What mattered was that my actions had implications that went beyond me and reflected negatively on my family.

This is the heart of the matter here. You represent all of the groups with whom you are associated. You represent your family, your school, your company and any number of other groups. Your behavior, positive and negative, reflects on these groups and their members as much as it does on you. Act honorably, and people will associate honor with the groups with which you are associated. Act dishonorably, and people will form negative opinions of these groups.

I felt honored when I was asked to contribute a few rules to this book. As a member of The Creating We Institute, I know that my writing reflects on all of my co-authors in this book as well as every member of the Institute. I feel a little extra responsibility to do the best job I can because of my responsibility to represent my friends and colleagues well. I want them to be proud of this book and those of us who contributed to it.

Sometimes things work out the other way. Several years ago the city of New York honored a group of policemen and firemen for acts of valor. After the ceremony, a few policeman and fireman over indulged a bit. What began as good natured bantering and taunting between New York's Finest (the police) and New York's Bravest (the firefighters) turned into a fist fight in front of a restaurant and bar that bordered one of the city's more popular parks. The incident was widely reported in the local papers and TV newscasts. Even though fewer than 20 cops and firemen were involved, none of whom were the honorees, both the Police Department and Fire Department suffered a big black eye. This negative public perception lingered until the bravery of both departments was displayed on 9/11.

If you want to behave in a WE-centric manner, you need to accept the fact that your actions are a reflection on you and on all of the people and organizations with which you are associated. Act in a manner that will reflect well on you and the others in your life.

22

Speak Your Vulnerable Truth

Charles Jones

Consider this scenario:

Although Phil was the logical choice for taking on a particular project, Jane was a bit wary of assigning it to him because he missed meeting the deadline on his last project. So instead, she assigned the project to Jim.

When Phil heard that the project had been given to Jim, he stopped by Jane's office and respectfully asked her why Jim had been delegated the project instead of himself. Jane assured Phil that he should in no way take this as a negative reflection on his abilities—she just simply wanted to give Jim a chance to expand his skills in this area.

On the surface, it might look like Jane was protecting Phil's self-esteem while getting the job done in the most expeditious way. However, it is interactions like this one that are the death of many a 'WE.'

By withholding the true rationale for her choice, and avoiding the real question, "why *Phil* didn't get the assignment," Jane was not candid with Phil. More likely than not, Phil picked up nonverbal clues of 'avoidance' at both the emotional and conversational level. Even if Phil doesn't know why Jane was being dishonest or hiding her true feelings, he will feel Jane's lack of honesty and candor. One 'small' incident like this can distort a working relationship. A series of such incidents can damage a relationship beyond repair.

At some level, we all know this. So why do we do it? Sometimes we hesitate telling the truth to people for fear we will hurt their feelings or ruin a relationship irreparably. Sometimes we don't tell the truth because we're not sure how.

To understand this dynamic more fully, let's replay Jane's situation from the top.

In this scenario, the first choice Jane faced was *what* to say to Phil when he missed the deadline on his last project.

Take 1: Jane could have asked Phil to recount the assessments and decisions he made that led him to miss the deadline. Having heard Phil's story, Jane would be in a better position to assess whether Phil could be trusted with projects such as these in the future. This kind of debrief is common in many organizations today and, although it may be preferable to doing nothing at all, it is likely to have a damaging effect on their relationship. Jane is, in effect, interrogating Phil with the assumption that Phil alone has something to learn from this experience. Imagine how this conversation would play out and how Phil might feel at the end.

Take 2: In contrast, Jane could have begun by acknowledging that since she delegated this assignment to Phil, both she and Phil were accountable for ensuring that the deadline was met. With this declaration of shared accountability, Jane and Phil could work together to unearth the various assessments and decisions that each of them made that led to Phil missing the deadline. How differently do you imagine this conversation would play out?

I'm guessing that Phil would not only feel more open to talk and identify things he could have done differently, but that Jane too would also identify one or more moments when she might have intervened in a helpful way. Both Phil and Jane would emerge from the conversation feeling empowered and far more connected. The rub, of course, is that in order for conversations such as these to happen, Jane must risk being emotionally vulnerable with a subordinate.

And yet, the benefits of relating to others through shared accountability and openness far outweigh the risks. Not only does this way of relating improve performance, it also strengthens the WE and leads to a far more humane workplace.

Practice Presence

Catherine Mullally

It is the ability to focus our attention that raises capacity and productivity and signals to others that we are engaging with our whole self.

A CEO walks into an emergency meeting with her executive team; the FDA has recalled their marquee product. The CEO, normally calm, is distraught and her team quickly mirrors that attitude. The VP of Public Affairs begins the discussion and, for the next fifteen minutes, the Chief Executive doesn't hear a word. Her mind is speeding around the variables, the stock price, the legal liability and how this could have happened to her.

What happens when a leader shows up but is not truly present? In this case, lack of CEO presence caused the team to shore up the walls between them, as each sought to avoid blame. The meeting dissolved without a plan, and the team left feeling suspicious of one another. What might this meeting have looked like if the CEO had practiced presence?

Presence is a skill, like any other we might acquire in our lives. Most executives work quite hard to develop the business skills necessary to run an enterprise. Very few take the initial step of examining their capacity to stay in the moment. Presence is not a mystery, nor does it require a specific background. Great leaders in all domains know the power of presence and use that capacity to perform at levels far beyond average achievement.

It's hard to imagine Tiger Woods making that final, perfect putt if his mind were occupied elsewhere, or Barack Obama engaging heads of state while his attention was diverted by other matters. Yet in business, we live under the myth of multi-tasking for higher productivity. In fact, it is the ability to focus our attention that raises capacity and productivity, and signals to others that we are engaging with our whole self. When we experience this in a leader, we become encouraged to participate similarly, which is what shifts the business into a WE-centric environment. By consciously developing Presence, a leader can turn a team of individual 'I's' into a higher order of co-creators equipped to guide an organization forward.

How can we train ourselves and others to stay present?

- **Quiet the Mind:** Like any skill, practice does make us better. Find a place that is quiet and comfortable. As a goal, hold a quiet mind for a count of five. Keep the spine straight, feet flat on the floor and with eyes closed, simply watch as thoughts come in and out of the mind. Instead of following the thought, have the intention to release them the moment they arise. When we quiet our thoughts, we become masters of our own mind. We are more present to others when we become more present to ourselves.
- **Practice Attention:** There are many ways to develop Presence and almost all of them include practices of concentration and observation. Find the one that works best for you—Meditation, Yoga, and Breathing.
- **Cultivate Wisdom:** Wisdom requires self-curiosity, the desire to understand who we are and how we frame our experiences so we are much more able to understand and accept the wisdom of others. Wisdom is contagious and when a leader makes this commitment, others will follow.

What is the impact?

- Greater creativity, as the leader avoids imposing old frameworks on new issues
- Increased capacity to shift out of deductive reasoning into a more right brain, intuitive knowing
- Open engagement among people resulting in heightened WE-centric collaboration
- A greater sense of personal calm, confidence, and congruence that generates the same in others

The following week, our CEO re-grouped with her team. Through practice, she was learning how to still her mind and encouraged her team to do the same. They made it through the product recall as a cohesive team; they acted as a WE, instead of a group of disconnected individuals, protecting their individual turfs. They bonded together, used their collective wisdom, and identified not just solutions but ways to provide additional and unanticipated value to their consumers.

Imagine what practicing presence can do for you, your team, and your organization.

Section V
Understand When to Pull Instead of Push

- Rule 24: Move With, Not Against, Partners
- Rule 25: Seek Engagement, Not Compliance
- Rule 26: Listen to Connect
- Rule 27: Embrace Different Perspectives
- Rule 28: Synergize Your Teams

24

Move With, Not Against, Partners

Judith E. Glaser and Jerry Manas

Rather than demanding others to step into a power-fight, we can request that others move into a power-with dance with us.

We interact energetically with others. We either move towards others, away from others, with others or against others. When we believe that others are our adversaries, we move against them. Action—reaction, tit-for-tat or retaliation, can transform them into adversaries.

Anthropologists and biologists believe we have a tit-for-tat instinct hard wired into our DNA. In fact, this instinct is evolutionary and is found in all mammals. Such is true, for example, when someone comes at us 'mammals' in anger, we fire off fear signals in our amygdala—a tiny organ found in the lower part of our limbic brain—and we move into our protection mode.

As soon as we see and feel the signals that someone is on the attack, we respond instinctively to protect ourselves. Some people react by matching anger with anger, often causing a fight to ensue. Others may flee if they feel the anger and aggression will lead to danger, believing that running away will save them from being 'eaten alive.' Others will freeze, hoping the aggressor will change their mind and move on to more enticing prey.

This dance of engagement drives all of human behavior. Psychiatrist Stuart Brown gives an incredible presentation that puts these interaction dynamics into context. Brown describes a meeting between an enormous 1,200-pound male polar bear and a female husky. The scene is the moment of contact between the two the polar bear and husky on the Hudson Bay in late fall, just north of Churchill, Manitoba.

In his constant pursuit of food, the polar bear focuses his predatory gaze onto the female husky, catching her stare. Under normal circumstances, the polar bear's generally fixed, rigid, and stereotypical behavior would end with the husky as his next meal, but this time, something unusual happens. The husky returned his gaze with an engaging and graceful bow and a wagging tail. The polar bear stood towering over the husky, and instead of claws and fangs, they began to engage in an incredible ballet.

This unexpected interaction is just as much a part of nature's order as the anticipated battle-to-the-death. Yet this time, it manifests as an incredible duet between predator and prey, with two animals in a transformed state a state of play. All because of the way the husky acted.

What trumps what in nature? We assume power over others gets us our way. And what is our way anyway? The dance in nature we witnessed in the story of the husky and the polar bear is a perfect example of how human beings and all other animals communicate. We send all types of signals all the time. We test each other—as the husky did the bear, and we see what comes back. Our signals work like radio signals saying: "Where are you?" and "What do you want?"

Our signaling system—what we send and what we receive—alerts us to the nature of our relationship with others. We either move towards others, away from others, with others or against others. Each signal generates a reaction that is as hardwired in nature as the fight-or-flight syndrome.

In our brains, we translate these signals into labels about our power relationship to others. We are either in a power-over or power-with mode of interaction with those around us. The husky's signals to play—power-with—trumped the polar bear's signals to dominate—power-over—certainly a trump that is one of nature's big surprises.

The antidote to the common power-over behaviors at work is to resist giving back power to others, and instead, request that they move with us into a power-with dance, thus avoiding the power-fight all together.

Antidote: Make requests, not demands. By moving toward and with others, with the intention of creating a greater, more engaging and (in business) a more productive outcome—our adult form of play can produce unimaginable and positive results. Our beliefs drive our intentions, our intentions drive our actions, and our actions drive the results we achieve with others.

25 Seek Engagement, Not Compliance

Jerry Manas

Many organizations implement some new process or form and wonder why people don't comply. Worse yet, instead of attempting to learn the newly proposed system, people instead grumble and spread the misery around the office. A better method for implementing such change is to engage people in co-creating the solution wherever possible. By soliciting feedback and presenting challenges for people to address, you'll be surprised by the ingenuity displayed and the level of participation. Next time, seek engagement instead of compliance, and see the difference it makes.

One of my coaching clients (let's call him Dave) was having difficulty getting his small staff of three to comply with using a new project management template he had recently implemented. "They don't seem to seem to appreciate the fact that I know this stuff better than they do," Dave lamented. "Besides, I know what's right for the organization—I've been doing this for 20 years!" Then he posed his question to me. "How do I get them to comply?"

I suggested that perhaps an alternate perspective of the question would be: "What objectives are we trying to achieve and how can I get people engaged in meeting the objectives effectively?" I added that it's not a matter of who knows what; it's a matter of how we engage others, how we communicate our needs to them, and how we meet *their* need for inclusion. I suggested he hold a meeting with the three people in question, with the following agenda and guidelines.

- Review the problem or opportunity that the template was meant to serve.
- Ensure that everyone agrees that the problem or opportunity is real and needs to be addressed in some manner. *If there is disagreement, try another perspective—that of meeting the needs of all parties in the room.*
- Review each element of the template in question and the need it is intended to meet.
- Have an open dialogue on alternate ways of meeting those needs, letting the staff take the lead and discuss alternatives. Avoid steering or directing the conversation at all costs.
- Be open to removing elements where the cost in confusion or time is not worth the value it brings. Try to integrate the ideas of all parties where possible.

Dave did hold the meeting with his staff, and reported back to me the following week. "Not only did we come away with a more streamlined and more effective template," he said, "but two members of my staff told me privately the next day that it was the first time since they've been with the company that they felt important." He almost seemed surprised. "They came in to thank me," he added. "In fact, the whole dynamic in our department has changed."

This did not surprise me in the least. I've seen similar results time and time again when people are included in the creation of outcomes, instead of being asked to comply with something that was inflicted upon them. The reverse is also true. I've seen countless organizations implement bureaucratic, laborious processes without the involvement or the engagement of the people who must use them, and they wonder why there's very little adoption of the new standards.

People need to feel included. They need to know what's in it for them and they want to have a say in how they do their jobs. Presentations, training, mission statements, road shows, lectures, or even audits, will not make people embrace anything and in fact some may even work to sabotage the new idea. Instead, we must engage people in co-creating methods and outcomes.

Listen to Connect

Lisa Giruzzi and
Judith E. Glaser

Listening to connect allows for a different level of conversation, where colleagues are enlivened, and energized; where creativity and innovation abound; and where people are forever changed.

Listening is a very complex process. Think about your last really great conversation. What made it great? Was it the speaking or the listening or some combination of both? Typically we do not give listening much thought and, if we do, the main concern is whether or not *we are* listening. The reality is that *how* we listen shapes and influences everything we encounter.

The traditional, 'I-Centric' approach to listening is primarily to listen for information, a transactional experience of asking and telling, each person delivering a monologue to their audience. Experientially, we feel left out, talked *at* and disconnected.

To create WE, one must **listen to connect**. Listening to connect brings people into our lives in a meaningful way by promoting mutual sharing and discovery. There is a sense of being talked *with*, and included in the process.

Listening to connect is not about waiting for others to stop talking. It's about being engaged in a discovery process, and anticipating what 'pearls of wisdom' will be shared or discovered. It's about quieting your internal dialogue and being fully present—generating acceptance, safety, and appreciation while others speak; and it's about allowing brilliance to emerge. Listening to connect allows for a different level of conversation, where colleagues are enlivened, and energized by each other; where creativity and innovation have a chance to emerge; and where people 'just might be forever changed.'

A powerful example is Corey, who despite being a very capable and skilled vice president in a financial company, was facing termination due to his negative impact on colleagues and clients. Corey was a talker; he talked about himself non-stop. He talked about his opinions, accomplishments, and contacts, never leaving a moment for another to interject. He thought of himself as a great communicator, never at a loss for words. Others viewed him as egotistical, boorish, and self-centered with no hope for improvement.

The damaging effects of his interactions were far reaching because of his high-level position; his colleagues and clients had no interest in working with him. The CEO gave Corey the option to either participate in executive coaching or be fired.

Through coaching, Corey learned the impact his 'I-centric' listening style was having on everyone, including himself. It was life changing. He began to notice the balance between listening and talking within a conversation. He became interested in *what he was listening for,* rather than listening for "how to win points." He began listening for how he could connect with people. Not only did this shift in listening alter Corey's ability to perform, but it also transformed the perceptions others had of him. Ultimately, he became someone who was well liked and admired by both his colleagues and clients and the CEO asked him to stay on at the firm.

Some principles of listening to connect are:

- Quiet your inner dialogue and focus your attention on the person speaking.
- Determine what judgments and opinions you are bringing to the conversation, then decide which you want to let go.
- Ask yourself *what you are listening for.*
- Before speaking, consider: "Have I fully understood this person's perspective?" If not, ask questions to gain more understanding.
- Listen for what you have in common; where you can agree and where new intersections can be born.
- Expect the person speaking to say great things; expect that you will say great things too.
- Share stories of your experience rather than just opinions.
- Appreciate the other person's point of view and thinking style.
- Notice the balance of speaking and listening.

Listening to connect has such extraordinary power that it can turn foes into friends and distrust into trust, one conversation after another. Opening ourselves up to notice our listening patterns can have a life-changing impact on everyone involved. As we listen to connect we are building a web of connectivity and expanding our circle of colleagues and friends. People will feel included and honored and will naturally want to give back as much, or more, than they receive.

Embrace Different Perspectives

Lisa Giruzzi

An atmosphere where it is safe to express different points of view and where there is freedom to dissent fosters powerful collaborative relationships

Each individual brings their own unique perspective to everything they encounter. Our perspective or point of view determines the world we see and experience. No two perspectives are exactly the same because each of us develops our perspective over time based on our past history.

In the traditional 'I-centric' paradigm, the 'game' is typically to seek out others who share a similar point of view. When we encounter those with differing points of view, we have two choices: to change their mind to agree with ours or to prove them wrong. This is all in an effort to protect our understanding of the situation (or of life). Why does our view need protecting? Winning is a primary objective of the 'I-centric' paradigm and being right equals winning. Proving others wrong is necessary in this right/wrong-win/lose approach to life, and being proven wrong is to be avoided at all costs.

Creating WE is a totally different game. A fundamental principle of creating WE is that all perspectives are valid; not right or wrong. In fact, embracing diversity of perspectives is essential for creating WE. A healthy WE is one in which all of the members' individual perspectives have been explored and considered by the group as a whole. This ensures everyone feels heard, which is critical for maintaining WE. Whatever decision is ultimately made, the decision makers have had the benefit of everyone's best thinking. Each 'I' within the WE can contribute to this goal by making sure they balance the amount of time they spend advocating their own point of view, with the amount of time they spend inquiring into the perspective of others—including drawing out the perspectives of those who haven't said anything.

When we honor diverse perspectives, and appreciate members for their contributions, we increase the likelihood everyone will embrace a new innovative strategy. WE-centric cultures create an atmosphere where it is safe to express differing points of view. Allowing for freedom to dissent fosters powerful collaborative relationships.

In one instance, three non-profit organizations were each working to develop their own individual events that would raise funds and also attract a larger donor base. When these agencies became aware of their common causes, interests, and goals they decided to work together and pool their resources. Unfortunately, after months of meetings and other efforts, there was little progress. Those involved were feeling frustrated and began to question whether deciding to work together was a good idea.

An intervention was arranged with the objective of moving the project forward. Initially, each of the organizations advocated for its own point of view and unintentionally dismissed those belonging to others. Additionally, each privately harbored the concern that their blended efforts would result in their own organization losing control of the project.

The intervention allowed for these fears to be identified and established a safe environment, which allowed for the differing perspectives on how to best achieve the goal to be shared and heard without judgment. After the right/wrong paradigm was left behind, the organizations were able to form a true collaboration and easily develop ways to work together to accomplish their goal. Within five months of the completion of the intervention, the inaugural event was held—over $55,000 had been raised for the cause.

Embracing different perspectives takes a willingness to give up being right about your own point of view, a commitment to inquire into the perspectives of others and an understanding that the benefits of divergent perspectives far outweigh any discomfort that one may encounter in the process of acknowledging them.

Synergize Your Teams

Josephine Washington

It takes courage to see more than the outer shell of a person and journey inward to inspire their hearts, minds, and souls.

Bill, the company's CEO, determined that it would need to shut down the business, effectively diminishing the livelihood of hundreds of families unless they were able to increase production, improve quality, and reduce staff costs. They were at the pivot point: change or die!

Over the years, they had conducted several high performance training programs for the teams, but nothing changed. Bill declared that the supervisors—not the team—were the problem. He decided to give training one more try, but this time it would be for the team and providing them with additional training would be a fix for the "hard hat, steel-toe shoe wearing guys."

Even though he was not convinced that supervisory training would work, Bill brought in Joyce, a training consultant, as one last attempt to create change. He let Joyce know that he really didn't think the supervisors would ever change their unproductive behaviors; he just couldn't see it. But as one last effort to save his company, he challenged her to get results. He also 'kindly' informed her, "We have fired three other training consultants before you. Good Luck!"

Six months later, to his pleasant surprise, Bill started noticing behavior shifting among the supervisors: positive interactions, dramatically improved attendance at meetings, more interest in performance results, and eager learners who sought to work as team players. Everyone noticed!

Four months later, Bill was reviewing the third quarter performance reports. To his utter amazement, productivity and quality levels had increased significantly. Unable to contain his enthusiasm, he immediately made a call to Joyce: *What's going on?*

Joyce and her colleague Cheryl prepared their presentation, which included her belief that leaders have the critical responsibility to create a synergetic organizational culture that inspires open learning and WE-centric principles. Like great athletes and musicians, the performance of the supervisors depended upon their emotional, mental, and spiritual preparation to work in an inspiring environment.

Joyce decided to present her plan to establish the Synergy Zone on the shop floor where the supervisors were inspired to discover their inner strengths, share new knowledge, and unearth the team's wisdom. Practicing these synergizing team techniques weekly, wisdom emerged. Supervisors became focused, competent, and passionate about a greater purpose other than themselves. When an egg is sitting still, it can be easy to forget that inside it is still something very special developing. It takes courage to see beyond the outer shell of a person and to journey inward to inspire their hearts, minds, and souls. Joyce closed the presentation with some helpful tips. The APPLY® Invitation coaching development principles were ideal.

The simple principles for APPLY® Invitation are:

Authentic-Self	Appreciate and honor your inner self. Understand your personal unique gifts, talents, and abilities.
Purpose	Deepen your inner knowing of your personal destiny. Align your aspirations to advance your personal and professional goals.
Practice	Implement inspired actions to promote your learning opportunities. Realize the power of practicing often.
Learn	Build your knowledge and skills to increase your performance capabilities. Open your heart and mind to explore new horizons.
Your Growth	Share your learning experiences and your wisdom will emerge. Commit to sharing and nurturing your positive development continuously.

Instantly upon stepping into Bill's office, she knew something different was going on. His desktop was totally cleared and he was completely focused. Bill began telling Joyce about what he had been observing and learning as though he had read her presentation notes.

Without a doubt, Bill was very much in rhythm with "what was going on." Joyce discovered that Bill too was inspired by his supervisors and had learned the value of the synergizing team practices. Bill soon became a highly respected leader and began advocating to other executives around the world how inner wisdom synergizes teams. The company remains open today and is operating with a high degree of success.

Section VI
Realize How Words Create Worlds

- Rule 29: Create Shared Meaning
- Rule 30: Support Others in Recognizing Needs
- Rule 31: Separate Opinions from Facts
- Rule 32: Be Willing to Change Our Beliefs
- Rule 33: Advocate for Needs, Not Means
- Rule 34: We Are What We Write
- Rule 35: Be Elegantly Inclusive

Create Shared Meaning

Lisa Giruzzi

Simple everyday terms such as teamwork, leadership, and respect have entirely different meanings depending on whom you talk to.

"Language is the house of Being; in its home man dwells. Those who think and those who create with words are the guardians of this home."
—Martin Heidegger, German philosopher, *Letter on Humanism*, 1947

Words, words, words. We are surrounded by words. We think in language, we speak in language, we read and write in language and yet we take language for granted. We spend little to no time actually distinguishing what we *mean* by the words we use in communication with others.

A fundamental assumption is that we all mean the same thing when we use the same words, despite the fact that virtually all words have more than one meaning and can even have totally different meanings depending on the context. Given our diverse backgrounds and perspectives, is it surprising that we have different interpretations of what words mean?

In order to create WE, shared meaning of common language must be established. For instance, if an organization has a set of guiding principles or values, effort must be made to ensure everyone has a shared understanding of this meaning.

An office equipment company experienced this dilemma first-hand. One of the tenets of their business was providing excellent customer service. This company was made up of a sales team and a technical support team. The sales team was responsible for all aspects of sales while the technical support team was responsible for the setup and service of the machines that the company sold.

The owners of the company were distressed by ongoing reports of mediocre service by customers. In spite of the owners' persistent efforts to emphasize excellent customer service with their employees, there was no change. The need to create shared meaning was discussed with the owners. Their response was, "Everyone knows what it means."

Contrary to the owners' assertion this was not the case. The sales team defined excellent customer service as forming relationships with the customers and making sure they were taken care of. It entailed lots of communication and 'schmoozing.' On the other hand the technical support team defined it as getting the machines running as quickly as possible. In fact they felt that communication with customers should be kept to a minimum, concentrating only on the facts.

This example may sound extreme but it is far more common than you think. Simple everyday terms such as teamwork, leadership, and respect have entirely different meanings depending on whom you talk to. If you have teenagers at home, you know your definition of 'clean' often does not match theirs. Coming to a shared understanding can avert conflicts and all sorts of negative consequences.

Some ideas for creating shared meaning are:

- Ask people to share examples rather than definitions. For example, can you tell me a story of a time when you provided excellent customer service?
- Assume your definition of words differ from others' definition.
- Respect others' interpretations. They have valid reasons for *their* definitions.
- Ask, "What do WE mean by _____?"
  Be willing to create your own unique definition. While there may be similarities, a baseball team has a distinct definition of team that is different from a crew team, or from a sales team.
- Don't be afraid to use enough words to say what you mean. Everything does not need to fit on a bumper sticker.
- Keep asking questions until you are confident that you have created shared meaning.

In order to create WE, the members need to know what they are a part of. That can only happen when there is a shared understanding of what things mean.

30 Support Others in Recognizing Needs

Nancy Ring

We can invest our energy in helping people get their needs met and see them be effective and productive, or we can ignore those needs and deal with people's reactive and ineffective stress behavior.

Despite what many businesses would like to believe, we humans all have core needs—from the way we need to be treated to the elements in our lives that feed us.

Businesses often worry that acknowledging those needs will require extra resources and have a negative impact on the bottom line. "Paying attention to individuals' needs just seems like too much work," managers can complain. In reality, though, we have two choices: we can invest our energy in helping people get their needs met and see them be effective and productive, or we can ignore those needs and deal with people's reactive and ineffective stress behavior.

Either way, it's an investment. Personally, I'd much rather support people's effectiveness than put up with their stress. More times than I can count, I've seen it pay off in organizations as well.

A large pharmaceutical company in Minneapolis is a great example. The issue is that their efforts to get their new treatment for rebuilding weakening bones through the R & D process were floundering. Conflicts were afoot between the leader of the Osteoporosis Therapeutic Area, Dr. Simpson, and his scientific team. As the timelines tightened, they fell further and further behind and their data continued to look less and less promising. The scientists were better at undermining each other's results than they were at developing credible results of their own.

"The stress is killing us," Dr. Simpson told us. Frustrated that people were not able to work together, he set up three data review meetings a week where people were forced to present and defend their data in the face of the harshest of criticism.

The effect, however, was less progress, lower productivity, and more conflict about how to approach scientific dilemmas. Half of the group was so busy trying to get out of the meetings unscathed that they were not saying what they really thought about the science. The other half took the "best defense is a good offense" approach, ripping data sets apart without offering any solutions.

"You may work best in rigorous, large group debates," I told Dr. Simpson, "but it's clear that only a few on your team have that same need." We then worked with Dr. Simpson and his group to help everyone recognize and meet their own needs. During this process, we discovered that some team members worked better on their own, while others preferred to work in groups.

Some of the scientists wanted the team to structure their work, while others wanted to provide that structure themselves. A few of them wanted to continue the rigorous group debates, but those who learned better from one-on-one coaching and feedback were afforded that approach.

We led the team through a collaborative planning process where they created a strategy that factored in everyone's needs, not just Dr. Simpson's. The new approaches worked. Less than a month later, the Osteoporosis team was seeing promising data and their compound is now in clinical trials.

By recognizing and supporting the varying needs on his team—including his own—Dr. Simpson created an environment where the WE became bigger than the sum of the I's. And it looks like those who suffer from osteoporosis will benefit from this approach too.

31 Separate Opinions from Facts

Charles Jones and Whitaker Raymond

Treating opinions and facts as one and the same increases the risks of wounded egos....

More often than we realize, we argue about opinions as if they are facts. And when this happens, the quality of communication drops dramatically.

Julie, a senior executive of a financial services firm, was frustrated with her number one manager, Fred, who was in charge of relationship management with all important outside vendors.

Julie: "Fred, you are not close enough to our vendors. They don't know where they stand with us."
Fred: "Wait a minute, that's not right! I have communicated closely with them. Relax. Everything is ok."
Julie: "You don't understand," she quickly responded.

In the example above, Julie is expressing her views as if they are facts, as we all do on occasion. She talks with Fred as though she knows the truth—what actually happened and why. She's 'interpreting' what is happening with judgment—is already locked on what the situation and solution are.

Yet she (and others) might reach a different conclusion or opinion in the conversation had the facts been explicit and not assumed. As a result, Fred responds defensively—and shoots back an opinion of his own. For a few minutes they battle over these opinions until it is clear the conversation is only getting worse.

By themselves, opinions are not problematic. Why? Because our opinions are what move us to action—they are conclusions, judgments, and positions that we adopt after making meaning from observations and facts. What is problematic is misinterpreting or misrepresenting these opinions as facts, especially when they are judgments about others' actions.

Treating opinions and facts as one and the same increases the risks of wounded egos, strained relationships, wasted time, divisive conflict, and faulty decision-making. The degree of risk will depend on factors such as the level of agreement or disagreement, the relative organizational positions, and attitudes toward each other.

So, how can you avoid this mistake?

Precede your opinions with phrases like "Based on the facts I've heard, it's my opinion that ..." In the conversation above, Fred finally asked Julie, "Who specifically has said to you they don't know where they stand?" and the conversation shifted to focusing on Julie's previous observations.

Be explicit about your opinions on the issue, e.g.: "Fred, given my past conversations with a number of vendors, it's my opinion that you are not close enough to them."

Share your fact-based rationale for your position, e.g., "Fred, last week in a phone call with Bill Johnson and again yesterday in a meeting with Liz Gorning, they both said they weren't sure what to expect from us in the way of business in the months ahead. Bill said he is unclear what you want of his firm, and Liz was asking me a lot of questions about your view of relationships with firms such as hers. To me, this indicates they don't know where they stand, and it's possible that others are in the same boat too."

When you hear others stating their opinions as if they were facts, here are some ways you can encourage them to take ownership for their opinions:

Reframe their statement as an opinion and reflect it back to the group, e.g., "Julie, so you are of the opinion that there's a problem, and a serious one. How do we get at the facts here?"

Ask the speaker for their rationale, e.g., "I need to understand this better. What's happened that led you to this conclusion?"

Call out and/or challenge the speaker's [unspoken] assumptions, e.g., "Julie, this is a serious view you have, and therefore important. Are you concerned not just about the vendors but also about the way I am doing my job?"

Whatever approach you use, owning your opinions and helping others own theirs will minimize pointless battles of opinions, damaged egos, strained relationships, and faulty decisions. Done well, this simple act of acknowledging opinions reinforces an environment of trust and transparency, and strengthens the bonds of WE.

32 Be Willing to Change Our Beliefs

**Judith E. Glaser and
Jerry Manas**

Conversations, especially those where we are entrenched in our own view of the world, are rarely neutral.

We create WE through conversations. That may be a bold statement; yet when we think about it, it rings true. Conversations connect us to each other, and enable us to share and compare our views, feelings, insights, and wisdom. As we connect through conversations we move from the 'I' to a sense of 'WE.'

Conversations enable us to see how we are alike, and how we are different from others. Most of all, conversations enable us to see the world through each other's eyes, and to validate our perspectives of the world, a practice Marcus really needed to learn to be a great leader.

Marcus rose up the corporate ladder in marketing quite quickly, and in the process, he developed an edge of arrogance. His professional stature often went to his head, leaving him to believe his wisdom was invaluable. Consequently, during conversations with co-workers, he fell into the habit of making a point by correcting the other person's statements; it was subtle, yet unnerving for those around him.

Robert: I really think we need to rally the sales force by giving them new, glossy marketing materials they can leave behind with customers.
Marcus: Yes, but it's not really glossy that they need, it's really something that has a sense that we are launching a new product line. It's not glossy that we need.
Robert: What I want to do is get the sales force excited.
Marcus: Yes, but what they need is a message, not a glossy.

Marcus wasn't really listening. He used "Yes, but," a few too many times. Robert left the meeting feeling his perspective and his sales team's needs went unheard.

When our views differ from others, we often feel in conflict with them. Sometimes we can feel we need to argue for our perspective and convince others that our view is the right one. When we feel strongly about our views, we tend to focus more on persuading others to agree with our side and end up listening with deaf ears at what they are saying and what's important to them. We put our vested interests ahead of theirs.

Conversations, especially those where we are entrenched in our own view of the world, are rarely neutral. These conversations activate us emotionally, spiritually, intellectually, and physically. When we feel strongly about things, we fight for our beliefs, and try to influence others to bring them over to our side.

In healthy Co-creating Conversations®:

- We remain open to listening, we ask questions, we reflect on and ponder others' ideas, we engage to deepen our understanding of the situation, the person and the events.
- We recognize that we hold a strong point of view, but we remain open to learn and to determine if we need to change our view based on the new ideas and insights we are gaining.
- We exchange ideas, allowing influence to flow in both directions, even while we try at times to explain our own perspective; most of all we are open to influence.
- We acknowledge others' points of view, and we share our point of view like a conversational dance in an effort to discover the ways we interconnect and can co-create an even broader and more expansive point of view.

Some conversations, on the other hand, feel unhealthy. They feel very one-sided. When one person does all the talking, it feels like he or she is talking at, or down to, as opposed to 'with' the other person. In the worst-case scenario, it feels like he or she has stopped listening all together.

When we engage in conversations by *telling* others what's on our minds, we can come across as pedantic, controlling, and unwilling to change our beliefs. When we are open and generative—when both of us are willing to allow our words and beliefs to transform our think-ing—we rise up and create a bigger WE. When we are able to let go of vested interests, faulty assumptions, outdated beliefs, worn-out stories, and open our minds to new possibilities, we transform our re-lationships and our environments to ones that breed innovation, sus-tainable leadership and business success.

33 Advocate for Needs, Not Means

Charles Jones

Once John and Jane shift the focus of the conversation to their respective needs, they will immediately cease operating as adversaries and begin operating as partners.

We've all had the experience of seeing a WE devolve into two or more 'I's' due to seemingly irreconcilable differences of opinion on how to proceed. John from Engineering is certain that X is the only way to resolve the product issue but Jane from Sales is convinced that the customer will accept nothing short of Y.

This is a classic example of two parties, each of whom have legitimate concerns, locked in a dispute that offers little chance for a happy ending. If they move forward with X, Jane loses; if they move forward with Y, John loses; and if they reach a 'compromise,' both Jane and John will have lost.

The problem is that Jane and John are advocating for the wrong thing. Instead of advocating for the fulfillment of their respective needs, John and Jane have slipped into advocating for a particular means by which to meet their respective needs. And as long as the conversation continues to be framed in terms of these particular means (i.e., X and Y), there will be conflict, hard feelings, and sub-optimal outcomes.

However, once John and Jane shift the focus of the conversation to their respective needs, they will immediately cease operating as adversaries and begin operating as partners. Instead of advocating for X and Y, John will advocate for finding a solution that will not raise Engineering's unit cost while Jane advocates for finding a solution that will satisfy the client's standards for reliability. X and Y may still prove useful as starting points for the conversation.

For example, Jane may respond with a list of client needs that would not be met by X and John can responds with a list of engineering needs that would not be met by Y—opening a collaborative space in which Jane and John can work toward a breakthrough solution that meets both parties needs. Failing a breakthrough solution, John and Jane can use the dilemma to clarify the organization's priorities and values—and move forward with a Z that is a win for the WE of which John and Jane are now a part.

The next time you find yourself relating to someone in your WE as if they were a 'them,' check to see if the two of you are locked in an argument over means rather than a collaboration over needs. If the answer is 'yes,' try shifting the focus of the conversation from means to needs by saying something along the lines of:

"It seems like you want to find a solution that will address engineering's need to keep costs down while I want to find a solution that addresses our client's need for increased reliability. What ideas do you have for meeting both of these needs?"

If you don't know what needs the other party is trying to meet, ask:

"I'd like to find a solution that works for everyone. You've said that X would not work for you. Would you be willing to say what needs of yours would not be met by X?"

If you're stuck, think about how you could expand the WE:

"Who could help us generate some new ideas on this?"

"The client's engineer seemed to have a good grasp of the problem. Do you think he would be willing to work with us to find a solution?"

If this last suggestion sounds a bit unorthodox, consider the competitive advantages of operating a business in which your customers as well as your suppliers consider themselves part of the same WE.

34

We Are What We Write

Deborah Dumaine

We work so hard to create a positive relationship, but it can be damaged in a moment with a thoughtless message.

Creating a great organizational climate has a silent challenge: the written word. In this age of globalization, we have begun managing and collaborating more in writing and less in person. Your words represent you on computer screens 24/7. They should instantly evoke the warm and collegial WE relationships you desire. Your readers should feel your presence in print—the person behind the message, behind the business.

Sometimes we act with thoughtless urgency and write emails such as, "Where's my answer? Didn't you get my email?" Or we forget to add a friendly, human touch. The reaction to such a careless message can be fear or irritation, setting up the working relationship to fail. Cooperation and teamwork are successfully built on how you present yourself in the written word, especially today when we may never meet some of our colleagues face-to-face.

Which message would you prefer to receive?

- Your response to this problem was way off base!
- Can you explain this???
- Please help me to understand our handling of this issue.

Which encourages defensiveness? Which encourages collaboration and WE? We work so hard to create a positive relationship, but it can be damaged in a moment with a thoughtless message. The next time you write, try following the process below to create WE in your writing.

Begin with a plan

Before you start to write, focus on; Why am I writing? Do I have to ask for something or recommend something?

Then consider your readers: What information, and how much information, do they need from you, given what you want from them? A relationship is born—and it's WE, not ME.

Now write

Not from beginning to end, like a novel, but from what's important: what you want, why you want it, and so on. Your readers are in a hurry—don't ask them to spend time trying to understand your point.

What's in, what's out?

Give them everything they need and nothing more, except good manners: "Please," "Thank you," and a positive tone about the great results you'll achieve together. Where you've been bears mentioning, but only after words that inspire. What went wrong in the past is nothing compared to the steps leading to a better future.

Walk away—then come back

When you're done writing something important, re-read it, listening to your own voice. Did you speak with the kind of formality reserved for a state function? Or did you honor the relationship (the WE), by creating a level playing field with simple and direct words that allow your readers to sail through your message?

The final check

- Did you consider the relationship of your words to your venue: keywords for the web, acronyms defined as needed, and understandable abbreviations for texting and IM?
- Are your sentences long, passive, and full of ancient, worn-out phrasing like 'It has come to my attention'? Or are they active and mostly limited to two lines?
- Are your paragraphs six lines or fewer? If not, break them up; consider bullets, numbers, or links.
- Did you put vivid headlines above key paragraphs, such as 'Recommendation,' 'Suggested Deadline' or 'Action Requested'? Your headlines should tell the story.
- Spelling, grammar (including run-ons and passive voice), punctuation—check them all. Don't appear sloppy!

Message sent, relationship secure: You're done!

35

Be Elegantly Inclusive

**Charles Jones and
Whitaker Raymond**

**Seek 0% objection
NOT 100%
agreement.**

Sometimes meetings turn into unfriendly tennis matches, drawn out consensus building extravaganzas, and we can't see how to stop them without people feeling unheard or excluded.

Situation #1: Sharon was struggling to understand how she had become a spectator in a meeting she had called. She had asked the account manager and accounts receivable clerk to come by to discuss why the Ramsey account was six months overdue. All she really wanted to know was how they would prevent this from happening in the future. What she got instead of a decision, was an increasingly heated tennis match between the account manager and accounts receivable clerk about what the other should have done differently.

Situation #2: John invited his team of seven to participate in a decision. Truth is, this was his decision to make, and if he wasn't so worried about taking a beating on his next 360 for not being 'inclusive' enough, he would have made his decision and sent it out as an inform to the rest of the committee. He allocated 20 minutes to reach consensus and here they were, 40 minutes into the meeting still with no decision in sight. To kill some time, he calculated how much it was costing the company to have all seven of them in this room for an hour.

Situation #3: Jane was certain that if she heard yet one more person offer their rationale for why they supported Tom's proposal, she was going to scream! And yet she knew from past experience that if she interrupted the current 'love fest,' she would be accused of trying to railroad the meeting. If only someone would call her on her mobile so she could excuse herself from the meeting and get back to being productive! It is conversations like these that give 'WE's' a bad name. What's important to understand about these conversations is that there are really two agendas at work:

- Making decisions that enable the collective WE to move forward.
- Meeting the needs of the individual 'I's' to have their concerns considered and their ideas heard.

Failure to manage both agendas skillfully can lead to disintegration of the relationships among the 'I's' and/or failure of the WE to achieve its goals. Here are some tips for holding efficient meetings in environments that value both efficiency and inclusiveness:

- **Establish the decision to be made.** In the example above, Sharon was asking for trouble when she phrased the agenda item as "Discuss the Ramsey situation"—which opened the door for discussions about anything and everything.

  Instead, had Sharon phrased her agenda item as "Having discovered that the Ramsey account is six months in arrears, what actions will we take?" the meeting would have generated joint recommendations instead of destroying the relationships.

- **Clarify up front what input is expected.** In the example above, John framed the goal as reaching consensus—effectively ensuring a lengthy debate. Had he clarified up front that this was his decision and that what he needed was perspectives for influencing his decision, he might have avoided the conflicts. In reflection he realized that he didn't need input from two of the invitees and that the best way to gather this information from the remaining folks would be through one-on-one conversations.

- **Seek 0% objection NOT 100% agreement.** In the example above, Sharon could have turned her frustration into forward motion by asking: "Is there anyone who has an objection to moving forward with Tom's proposal?" If not, the discussion could move to next steps. If yes, people could spend their time coming up with alternative solutions instead of wasting their time 'piling on.'

Follow the recommendations above and you will be practicing the art of "being elegantly inclusive"—an increasing valuable skill in organizations that places a high value on both inclusion and efficiency.

Section VII
Expand Belief Systems and Perspectives

- Rule 36: Think and Act "BIG WE, little me"
- Rule 37: Trumpets for Success
- Rule 38: Look Back to Look Forward
- Rule 39: Look at WE, Not Me
- Rule 40: Focus On What Works
- Rule 41: Create a Shared Vision for the Future
- Rule 42: These are Our Rules. What are Yours?

Bud Bilanich

**While we all have
to take
responsibility for
ourselves and our
success in this
life, we need to do
so in a way that
honors the
various wholes of
which we are a
part.**

Thinking and acting "BIG WE, little me" is not
about denying yourself, your needs, or your individuality. It is about realizing that you are part of
a whole that is greater than you. We all are. We
are members of families, communities, work organizations and societies. While we all have to
take responsibility for ourselves and our success
in this life, we need to do so in a way that honors
the various wholes of which we are a part.

The I-centric thinking that led us into the greatest
financial crisis since the great depression is an
example of the opposite of this rule. It is "BIG
ME, little we" thinking to the maximum. "I'll get
mine; you need to watch out for yourself."

"BIG WE, little me" thinking on the other hand,
comes from a perspective of "We're all in this
together. I need to take care of myself in a
manner that enhances the greater good."

It's not easy to approach life from a "BIG WE,
little me" perspective. We see the exact opposite
every day. Companies play budgetary games.
They pay a premium for temporary workers who
fill necessary slots in their workforce. They do
this because temporary workers are a variable
cost that can easily be eliminated, and look
better on the balance sheet.

Managers argue among themselves about which
department should absorb costs that benefit the
entire organization. They do this because they
are more worried about their department's
budget performance than the financial perfor-

mance of their company. Individuals say things like, "It's not my fault, but it's hers. I sent her an email, she never got back to me with the information I needed to complete this assignment." They do this because they are more interested in their own performance rating than they are in the performance of their company.

These are real examples that play out every day in US companies, which are the result of "BIG ME, little we" thinking. It takes courage to change this type of mindset. It begins with personal responsibility. If someone doesn't respond to your request in a timely manner, call or visit him or her. Explain the urgency of your need. Help him or her understand. Offer to help him or her down the road. That's "BIG WE, little me" thinking in action.

In '42 Rules to Jumpstart Your Professional Success,' I discuss the importance of mentors and mentoring. Mentors, by definition, embody "BIG WE, little me" thinking. Most often they are successful people who are willing to give of themselves, their time and energy to help others learn and grow. Through their efforts, they not only help individuals develop and succeed, they strengthen their organizations and communities.

You can demonstrate "BIG WE, little me" thinking by becoming a mentor yourself. It's never too early to become a mentor. We all have something to give. The sooner you begin giving, the better. If you're in college, you can mentor high school students. If you're a recent graduate, you can mentor others still in school. If you've been in your job for a year or two, you can mentor a brand new colleague. Mentoring is a great way to serve others and your organization; and it is a great way to demonstrate your "BIG WE, little me" attitude.

In 'The Different Drum: Community-Making and Peace,' Scott Peck offers a great example of the "BIG WE, little me" concept. He calls it "true community," characterized by "deep respect and true listening for the needs of the other people." Notice that he does not suggest that people subjugate their own wants and needs, only that they pay closer attention to the wants and needs of the people around them. When you do this consistently, you are a "BIG WE, little me" person, and an asset to yourself, your organization, and your community.

37 Trumpets for Success

Jerry Manas

Isn't 'WE' really about people on a team having their priorities straight, whether or not someone is "steering the ship?"

When we think of organizations where the employees seem to share a similar attitude, and have their priorities clear, it's hard not to think of the Walt Disney Company. Anyone who has visited any of the Disney theme parks knows that a Disney cast member (as all Disney employees are called) is well-trained, courteous, always in character, and efficient. I often wondered what went on behind the scenes at Disney, so I decided to take some workshops with the Disney Institute.

There were a number of eye-openers, but one of the most valuable lessons was also one of the simplest. Instead of fancy and complicated policy manuals, Disney relies on simple things that stick in people's minds. One of these tools is what they call *prioritized service quality standards*. They are, in order:

- Safety
- Courtesy
- Show
- Efficiency

Disney cast members are taught that Safety trumps everything. Courtesy is the next most important priority. Cast members must be courteous, but not if it means overlooking safety. After that comes Show (i.e. being in character; and creating the perception that everything is real). It's important to maintain the Disney image, provided that it doesn't get in the way of safety or courtesy. Last, but still important, is Efficiency. Disney is known for their efficiency, but safety, courtesy, and show must come first. This simple list of priorities is instinctive to all Disney cast members.

Here's how this list might play out. If a child were about to fall from a platform, a Disney cast member would instinctively run to help, regardless of whether he or she was helping a guest, or had to go "out of character" to address the safety issue. Likewise, if a ride could be made more efficient but it would make the riders feel rushed, or would detract from the experience, the modification would be nixed by Disney.

As Disney knows, when people are immersed in their work, they are often too busy to remember complicated rules or mission statements. Instead they need a simple reminder of what the key priorities are that should guide their actions. Ideally, this should be no more than three or four items, in order of importance. This gives people real guidance when making independent decisions. And let's face it; we don't want people to be dependent on management for every decision.

When trying to achieve a WE-centric culture, it's important to drive consistent and value-driven behaviors, whether or not management is present. Such clearly defined and simple standards help guide people's actions and diminish the need to always ask a superior for directions.

Let's apply this concept to a software project for instance. Let's say we had a software development team and we had set three prioritized service standards:

- Ease of use
- Ease of maintenance
- Performance

Software developers would know instinctively what their priorities should be. The product must perform well, but not at the expense of being maintainable, and certainly not at the expense of being easy to use.

These are just a few examples of the many ways prioritized service standards can be more powerful than any mission statement. Such standards are simple, easy to remember, and above all, *actionable*. For far too long, we've relied on mission statements and value statements in a well intentioned attempt to create a WE spirit. But isn't 'WE' really about people on a team having their priorities straight, whether or not someone is "steering the ship?" Prioritized standards enable that to happen.

38 Look Back to Look Forward

Judith E. Glaser

When you are gazing back at your life, pay attention to finding experiences that inspire you with passion and excitement.

In what direction do we hold our vision? We have 360 degrees to work with, but where do we put our attention?

The study of attention, and how it impacts us every day of our life has been a life long fascination. New developments in neuroscience are giving us clues about attention that are suggesting how we use our attention can change the hardwiring of the brain radically and for the better. If we learn to pay attention to our attention, we can even create transformations that defy our greatest expectations.

My first lesson on attention came from Larry, a 24-year-old mentally challenged adult living at the Bess Stone Center, a residential home for mentally disabled adults in Lawrence, Kansas.

Larry and I met on my first day of work. He was very tall and very thin. Perhaps the most striking feature of his appearance was the wide suspenders he wore to hold up his pants. His teeth protruded and his head was oversized.

"His name is Larry," Mary Jean said to me. "He is 24 but has the mind of a 2-year-old." He doesn't talk, he just grunts. As she spoke those words, his head tilted and I immediately knew he understood her harsh words. Larry looked different, and even though his outward appearance was unusual, it was clear that there was much wisdom that lay beneath Larry's surface, a fact that I was about to learn.

Larry, who did not possess the ability to communicate through words with others, put his talents to work and made an invention. By inserting the 'foil' from the inside of a ketchup bottle top into a clothespin, Larry was able to gaze into the small foil 'rear view mirror' for a fully encompassing view of the world.

Larry used his invention and attention to watch the man who came to polish our floors once a week. Larry watched the up motion and the down motion in his mirror, and once his mind mapped the rhythm, he imitated floor polishing even when the polisher was not there. I asked him if he wanted to try it out and sure enough, Larry became the best floor polisher ever.

He polished floors every day. Then he took me outside and motioned with his arms he wanted to polish the grass. After it clicked in, I realized he wanted to transfer his new found skills to learn to mow the grass. And he did, he became the best grass mower we had ever seen!

Larry's energy and passion for learning became contagious. Soon enough, everyone became alive in a new way. Bertha wanted to play the piano, and she did, in her own way. Albert wanted to have 'money in his pocket' and so Mary Beth gave him money to carry to the store for food shopping. Mark wanted to build a house, and so we gave him wood to build a miniature house which upon its completion was donated by the Bess Stone Center to its 'sister home' for mentally disabled children. The local newspaper heard about the change at Bess Stone and came in to write a feature story, which went on to greatly inspire our small town in Kansas.

Larry taught us all about *looking back to look forward*. When you are gazing back at your life, pay attention to finding experiences that inspire you with passion and excitement—and lo and behold, they will help you attend to the future in new ways.

- Exercise your Looking Back to Look Forward skills with others.
- What you pay attention to drives your intention.
- Use your 360-degree mirror to find memories that ignite your passion.
- Share those memories with others, as Larry taught us to do, and watch your life transform.
- When we put our attention on what gives us passion, we catalyze growth in our selves and trigger the Growth Instinct in others.

39

Look at WE, Not Me

Jane M. Hewson

Team members excelled in their individual assignments because the definition for their success was shaped by connectivity and collective purpose.

Success is often measured by our ability to achieve goals while working with others. Yet when working in the context of a team, we still tend to perceive success using individual sets of criteria. In order to bridge this gap, WE-centric leaders must build frameworks for their teams that create tensile strength and establish fresh new benchmarks for success.

Learning to see the commonality of views and approaches in teams can be challenging for many of us. Even acknowledging that a team approach is more powerful than an individual approach can be difficult. Most of us come to each new business setting with a predisposition of what success looks like.

For example, the disciplines of Marketing, IT, Finance and Product Development often function in a parallel configuration. With traditional benchmarks, a Chief Marketing Officer may define success as increased market share. An IT head may define it as the successful launch of three technology support services. The CFO may tell you that cost containment means success. The product developer may label the introduction of three new consumer products as success. How can each discipline learn to see itself in the context of the other, and in the context of the goal they are all trying to achieve?

A management-consulting firm went about developing a new line of service for its clients in a powerful way. The senior management assembled a team of players across the five primary administrative disciplines. A project leader introduced the goals and market drivers of the new service branch to her colleagues. She asked each colleague to consider what their respective disciplines could contribute to the flow and quality of the service. From the outset, the project leader created a collective and balanced approach for the team, placing each participant on an equal footing, thus creating a WE-centric view of the assignment.

The project leader used a simple visual to represent the framework of the team: the hub and spokes of a wheel, a framework for programmatic planning that evenly weights all the disciplines at the leader's fingertips. The Hub-and-Spoke Approach© to teamwork places the client's need at the hub, from which radiate the creativity and skills provided by the team members responsible for successfully delivering the service.

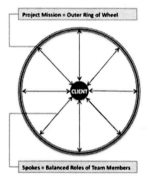

The teamwork graphic quickly communicated to each team member that success would be achieved by creating a balanced connection of viewpoints, all linked to the end client. Team members excelled in their individual assignments because the definition for their success was shaped by connectivity and collective purpose.

They were inspired to consider how their spokes related to others in the wheel:

- Am I placing too much weight on my viewpoint?
- Have I shaped my thinking to blend well with others?
- Am I providing adequate support?

I have heard said that teamwork is the fuel that allows common people to achieve uncommon results. Think of the tensile strength possible when leaders ensure that each team member sees success as evenly interdependent, drawing stability from multiple disciplines, and shifting their viewpoints from 'me' to WE.

40 Focus On What Works

Lisa Giruzzi and Nancy Ring

People are free to challenge themselves and give it their all.... Even failures occur differently; they go into the *potential success queue* waiting their turn to succeed.

At any given moment we can choose where we focus our attention and our energy. We can focus on what's working or what's not; our strengths or our weaknesses; what gives us energy or what drains it. We know intuitively that what we focus on grows. In other words, the more we give something attention, the more of it we see.

Have you ever bought a new car? Once you buy it, as if by magic, all you see are cars similar to yours. The fact is those cars were always there, you just didn't pay any attention to them. Here's another illustration of this concept: which would you rather have? The golf coach who tells you to hit the ball straight down the fairway or the one who says, "Don't hit it in the woods?" Great athletes focus on *making* the shot, not on *not* missing it.

Choosing to focus on what works has a very different impact on results and one's experience than the more traditional 'what's wrong' approach. When you focus on what works it creates an environment where people's strengths are maximized, thereby allowing them to build confidence and mastery. This boost in confidence increases willingness and ability to take risks which positively impacts innovation and creativity.

In this type of culture, people are free to challenge themselves and give it their all. People have permission to be great and allow others to reveal their own greatness. Even failures occur differently; they go into the *potential success queue* waiting their turn to succeed.

In this atmosphere, creating WE is natural. Individuals get to shine inside the WE. There is no defensiveness, no need to make others wrong because everyone is right when they are valued for their unique set of talents and strengths. People connect on a deeper level forming interdependent relationships, each able to see their essential contribution to the whole.

A civil litigation firm, which had been in business for nine years, was struggling to attract new clients and effectively manage the cases they had. Interviews of firm members revealed a deficit style of management that sought to 'improve weaknesses' to increase productivity.

Through coaching and training, we introduced and implemented an appreciative approach, which focuses on what works. Once they shifted their focus from weaknesses to strengths, they made huge strides.

The results were outstanding. Individuals identified their strengths and work was distributed accordingly. Attorneys then took on more of the work they loved, thereby increasing productivity. Additionally, the firm identified its strengths, which enabled them to distinguish their niche and dramatically increase their ability to attract new clients.

When everyone was enabled to focus on their strengths, the whole truly became greater than the sum of its parts. Conversely, trying to fix weaknesses lessened the whole's ability to function. Imagine an engine made up of faulty parts: it just won't run well.

Creating profound results can be as simple as shifting your focus from weaknesses to strengths. Here are some ways to do that:

Weakness-Focused	Strength-Focused
Focus on fixing 'what's wrong'	Focus on 'highpoint' stories; the ideal
Study failures to discover cause	Study success to discern what works
Work to improve weaknesses of individuals	Work to enhance strengths of individuals
Right/wrong management approach	Management open to explore various approaches
Individualistic/'I-Centric'	Interdependent relationships encouraged, 'WE-Centric'
Compartmentalized culture/silo	Members essential contribution to whole recognized
Energy spent avoiding what the organization doesn't want	Energy spent creating what the organization wants

Create a Shared Vision for the Future

Lisa Giruzzi

Creating a vision for the future is not just an exercise; it is critical to effecting change today.

The future you envision gives you your experience now. Imagine an all-expense-paid afternoon at the spa, and then imagine being at work. Each gives you a different experience in this moment. Creating a vision for the future is not just an exercise; it is critical to effecting change today.

How do you create a vision for the future that creates WE?

First, commit to involving people in a meaningful way from all levels of the organization. Whether you have everyone in the organization attend a vision creation session or have representatives from each department do so or do widespread surveys, whatever you choose, be as inclusive as possible.

Next, determine the strengths of your organization (see rule 40). Most organizations' visioning efforts fail because they create a vision that is dependent on fixing their weaknesses rather than focusing on enhancing or mastering their strengths. This approach leaves people feeling disempowered and needing to be 'fixed.' Conversely, when a vision is anchored in the strengths of an organization, but still a stretch, people have something to strive for and feel the vision is attainable because it is based on reality.

A powerful way to distinguish the strengths of an organization is by sharing highpoint stories, times when the organization excelled or there was an experience of truly "winning the game."

Look for the themes and patterns in those stories. What was true about all of them? What occurrence or experience do they have in common? These themes are the core strengths of the organization.

Once you know the strengths of the organization, ask the question, if we woke up five years (or ten years, etc.) in the future and we had mastered our strengths, what would be possible? What results would you have achieved? The answer to these questions is your organization's vision of the future. Be loud and proud about the future you create and make sure everyone in the organization fully understands its meaning (see rule 29 on Shared Meaning).

It is vital at this point to ask the members of the organization to declare their role in making this future a reality. Which of their strengths will they contribute to the whole? Human beings operate at their best when they feel a part of something bigger than themselves *and* they experience being integral to its realization.

Lastly, begin today to operate consistent with the future you created. Don't wait. Act as if the future has already occurred. *Remember the future we anticipate gives us our experience in the present moment.*

A statewide Human Resources association can attest to the benefits of creating a shared vision for the future. Prior to doing so they were struggling to maintain focus. The members of this organization were located throughout the state, some in very remote areas. To make matters worse, the bylaws required the leadership to change every two years. Consequently the thrust of the association changed with each new executive team. An intervention to create a new vision for the future was held that included a broad range of stakeholders from all areas of the organization.

The association engaged in the steps outlined in this rule and achieved magnificent results. The discovery of their core strengths clarified the direction they wanted to pursue. They began to focus on who they were and how they could amplify their core strengths. The ten-year vision they developed generated a new level of excitement, partnership, and focus; new structures were designed to ensure continuity. People began volunteering for committees, offering their unique talents and strengths to the organization. Several years have passed since this event, and they continue to be engaged and focused on achieving their shared vision for the future.

When you create a shared vision of the future, everyone pulls in the same direction. When people can see their role in the fulfillment of that future, you get the force of WE.

42

These are Our Rules. What are Yours?

Dale Kramer Cohen, Rami Glatt and Michelle Boos-Stone

WE-centric leaders who create their own rules bring themselves more fully to the table, elicit more from each team member, and collectively generate greater success.

You've completed learning 41 Rules and have discovered quite a bit about creating WE-centric organizations. Now it's your turn to take the mantle. How should you begin? How do you create a rule that's meaningful, relevant, and valuable? How can that rule optimally bring all citizens of your organizational community into WE?

As a leader, you've likely created WE many times within your team, unit, division, or organization *without even realizing it.*

You may have an intuitive sense of what transpired during a meeting that caused it to turn out successfully.

However, the value of reflection and the articulation of the exact nature of the catalysts that led to the positive outcome are often overlooked. The opportunity to think about those times and create a rule that works just for you is now.

The rules for creating your own rule are simple. There's only one: they come from you. WE-centric leaders who create their own rules bring themselves more fully to the table, elicit more from each team member, and collectively generate greater success.

A Process for Creating Your Own Rules

- **Think** of a moment when you've experienced the feeling of creating WE. Maybe it was by helping someone in your organization solve a problem, complete a small task, or accomplish the annual goal that you set for yourself and your team.
- **Reflect** on what happened to create the feeling of success. Write down several sentences (3-4) that describe what you did, and the impact. The next day, take another look at your description. What surfaces as the one or two most important factors that enabled you to create WE?
- **Create** a rule to recreate that experience. It might be expressed as: "Find Joy and Share it...(Yes, in the office)" or "Enthusiasm Elicits Electricity and Epiphanies."
- **Post it** on your computer; in your wallet; carry it with you—*It's yours!*
- **Practice** using it with one person, then a group, then a team.
- **Use it** as your divining rod to creating WE.

Reflecting on actions that have successfully stimulated your team fuels the creation of your own rule. Consciously practicing it, along with the other 41 rules, enables the WE-centric leader to empower deeper experiences and create fuller team member engagement, and results in team performance that you wouldn't have thought imaginable.

About the Editor

Judith E. Glaser

Judith E. Glaser is one of the most innovative and pioneering change agents and executive coaches in the consulting industry. She is an Organizational Anthropologist, and the world expert in WE-centric leadership—working at the intersection of leadership, brand and culture with a direct line of sight to the customer.

In 1980 she founded Benchmark Communications, Inc. (www.creatingwe.com) and in 2007 she co-founded The Creating We Institute, a research and development partnership (www.creatingweinstitute.com) with practitioners globally—dedicated to harvesting new forms of engagement and innovation in the workplace.

Judith is a sought after keynote speaker, and has appeared on NBC Today, FOX News, ABC, CNN, MSNBC, and is frequently quoted in the WSJ, and the New York Times. She is a master facilitator of leadership and organizational summits where leaders harness and accelerate their abilities to co-create, innovate, and differentiate themselves in the marketplace. She has published hundreds of articles on strategic leadership and two best selling books, Creating WE: Change I-Thinking to We-Thinking & Build a Healthy Thriving Organization and The DNA of Leadership, selected by both Forbes and Business Book Review as one of the top business books of 2005 and 2006. Creating WE won an AXION Leadership Award in 2008.

She is a Licensed HeartMath Provider, certified in over 14 Leadership Assessments, Certifies Coaches in Creating WE Practices and Co-creating Conversations®.

A Contributors' Background

Bud Bilanich

Bud Bilanich, The Common Sense Guy, is an executive coach, motivational speaker, author and blogger who helps his clients succeed by applying their common sense. He is the Official Guide for Executive Coaching at Self-Growth.com, and the Careers Group Coordinator at FastCompany.com. He is a member of Creating WE Institute, and the USA Today Small Business Advisory Panel. He writes the popular blog www.SuccessCommonSense.com.

Dr. Bilanich is Harvard educated but has a no nonsense approach to his work that goes back to his roots in the steel country of Western Pennsylvania. His approach to personal and professional success is a result of over 35 years of business experience, 10 years of research and study of successful people and the application of common sense.

Bud is the author of ten books, including '42 Rules to Jumpstart Your Professional Success,' where he presents his blueprint for career and life success:

- Develop your self-confidence.
- Create positive personal impact.
- Become an outstanding performer.
- Become a dynamic communicator.
- Become interpersonally competent.

His clients include Pfizer, Glaxo SmithKline, Johnson and Johnson, Abbot Laboratories, PepsiCo, AT&T, Chase Manhattan Bank, Citigroup, General Motors, UBS, AXA Advisors, Cabot Corporation, The Aetna, PECO Energy, Olin Corporation, Minerals Technologies, The Boys and Girls Clubs of America and a number of small and family owned businesses.

Bud is a cancer survivor and lives in Denver Colorado with his wife Cathy. He is a retired rugby player and an avid cyclist. He likes movies, live theatre and crime fiction.

Michelle Boos-Stone

Michelle Boos-Stone is a Global Business Strategist, working and learning in the field of organizational change and strategic dialogue for the past 18 years. Her work focuses around developing leaders at their core and managing change to produce outrageous possibilities.

Michelle's work typically centers around the top 10-20% of leadership within organizations, helping them to see things differently to realize new future possibilities. Her utilization of visual communication and facilitation enables her to bring a unique perspective to her client work.

Michelle's global consulting practice, Michelle Boos-Stone & Associates Inc., focuses on shifting current models of how we see the world to one of possibility. She feels that in order for us to change the future, we must change our thinking and be open to changing the conversation. Michelle utilizes the unique framework of brain-based learning research, learning and personality styles, impactful visuals, color theory, behavioral research and a fat dose of humor and insight to engage participants at their core.

Michelle's commitment is to grow leaders and individuals at every level and to have a great time doing it. She is a faculty member of The Creating WE Institute. She can be reached at mboos13@aol.com. Visit her website at www.michelleboos-stone.com.

Bruce Cryer

Bruce Cryer has spent the past thirty years researching and teaching innovative approaches to maximizing health and organizational performance. He was named President and CEO of HeartMath LLC in 2000, having helped launch the non-profit Institute of HeartMath with founder Doc Childre in 1991. For eight years prior, he served as vice president for a biotech company. Bruce was the key architect of programs that incorporate HeartMath's innovative biomedical research into practical tools and strategies to enhance health, performance, creativity, and productivity for both the individual and the organization. He is co-author, with Doc Childre, of the book 'From Chaos to Coherence: The Power to Change Performance.' He is also lead author of the 'Harvard Business Review article (July 2003),' entitled 'Pull the Plug on Stress,' and co-author of 'An Inner Quality Approach to Reducing Stress and Improving Physical and Emotional Wellbeing at Work,' published in 'Stress Medicine (1997).'

Bruce has successfully guided HeartMath programs at organizations such as Mayo Clinic, Duke University Health System, Stanford Medical Center, NASA Goddard Space Flight Center, Motorola, Hewlett-Packard, UCSF's Center for the Health Professions, Kaiser Permanente, Blue Cross Blue Shield, BP, Unilever, and dozens of hospital systems across the U.S.

Deborah Dumaine

Deborah Dumaine, Founder and President of Better Communications (http://www.bettercom.com), and a founding member of Creating WE Institute.

Deborah has been changing the way corporations write since 1978. She is

- the founder of Better Communications®-a national management training and consulting firm specializing in Reader-Centered Writing®
- the author of the best-selling books Write to the Top: Writing for Corporate Success (Random House) and the Instant-Answer Guide to Business Writing (iUniverse)
- the author of the business writing section of ManageMentor, Harvard Business School Publishing's on-line learning software
- an acknowledged pioneer in diagnostic writing skill development
- a contributor to the World Book Encyclopedia.

Deborah holds graduate and undergraduate degrees from Smith College and studied at the University of Iowa. She has also served on the Massachusetts Governor's Council for Women's Business Development.

Better Communications trains 5,000 people per year. With its headquarters in Waltham, Massachusetts, Better Communications' team of national consultants delivers in—house writing workshops internationally. They are redefining corporate writing as a tool to clarify thinking and drive action. Better Communications offers workshops in sales writing, technical/scientific writing, financial writing, procedure writing, writing constructive feedback, e-mail writing, writing presentation documents, communicating change, customer-service writing, grammar and basic writing.

Deborah E. Garand

Deborah E. Garand, President of Integrity Integrations
http://www.integrityintegrations.com believes that "the impossible is possible" if drive and desire are harnessed through conversations grounded in integrity, trust, transparency, respect and a concern for others as well as oneself. Strong, productive relationships and teams are built on the foundation of integrity and trust. As speaker, facilitator or executive coach, Deborah engages corporations, teams and/or individuals through an approachable, collaborative interactive dialog opening conversations helping to co-create future goals while building high performance teams bolted to a cultural foundation of Integrity.

Deborah has been published in Leadership Excellence, is a faculty member of The Creating We Institute, has lectured at numerous universities, taught college, been featured in a documentary and has a successful, in-depth and diverse background in business, sales, mediation, and a lifetime of studying and implementing successful leadership methodologies. She believes our ultimate happiness and success comes from "raising our bar" while harnessing mind, heart, body and soul.

In honor of Creating We, she wouldn't be who she is today without the love and support of her husband David and children, Morgan and Ian.

Lisa Giruzzi

Lisa has always had a strong desire to make a difference in the world. She is fulfilling that desire every day as the owner of her company, Transformational Conversations. Lisa has over 20 years of experience in coaching and consulting others. She has helped thousands to transform their lives, realize their goals, and achieve more satisfaction and fulfillment. Lisa is passionate about causing a positive revolution in change.

Lisa is an accomplished speaker captivating audiences at workshops, keynotes and seminars nationwide on topics such as leadership, motivation, effectiveness, communication, team building, networking and customer service. Lisa's programs are life-changing and consistently receive the highest ratings from participants.

Lisa is a founding member of The Creating WE Institute, and a co-owner of Appreciative Inquiry Consulting, LLC; a consortium of consultants offering a collaborative, strength-based approach to strategic change and transformation.

Lisa co-hosts Real Conversations, a topic-driven television talk show dedicated to enhancing the quality of people's lives.

For more resources to transform your life or to sign up for Lisa's electronic newsletter visit www.transformationalconversations.com.

Rami Glatt

Rami Glatt is a student at Yeshiva University where he is a member of its Jay and Jeanie Schottenstein Honors Program. A Psychology major with a minor in Business & Administration, Rami has plans to pursue a doctorate in Industrial-Organizational Psychology and will be a visiting student at Columbia University during the Fall '09 semester.

Rami first came into contact with The Creating WE Institute when he was introduced to its founding member and CEO of Benchmark Communications, Inc. Judith E. Glaser. Since then, he has been heavily involved with the research and editing of Mrs. Glaser's upcoming book Change Your Conversations, Change Your Relationships, Change Your Life! He has also served as the assistant editor for The '42 Rules for Creating WE.'

An avid fan of all that is musical, Rami plays several instruments and is currently the keyboardist for Yaakov Chesed, a Jewish rock group (www.yaakovchesed.com).

Rami would like to thank his family, friends, and professors for their ongoing encouragement and support. He particularly wishes to thank Judith E. Glaser and Dale Kramer Cohen for their guidance and direction while working on this publication.

Jane M. Hewson

Jane Hewson is Principal of Beresford Partners, LLC, a consulting firm focused on improving the bottom line of privately held business operations. Her career spans over 30 years counseling leading companies on client development, marketing and communicating. Her focus has been on the unique issues challenging firms in the professional services arenas, including financial services, consulting, and the law.

Prior to establishing Beresford Partners, Jane served as CMO of Weil, Gotshal & Manges, and for 20+ years owned, and operated as Principal, Hewson Group Ltd., a marketing communications and client development consultancy.

Jane's work increasingly centers on helping clients learn to be successful face-to-face communicators. She was recently a guest on Lori Sackler's radio show "The M Word: Money and Families," http://www.wor710.com/pages/2658881.php, to discuss ways in which family members can be more comfortable speaking with one another about personal finances, and interviewed about "The Real Art of Listening" by Colin Goedecke for his blog series on helping us think, act and communicate in wiser ways, www.tenowls.blogspot.com.

She is a founding member of The Creating WE Institute, www.creatingweinstitute.com. Her current professional pro bono work is dedicated to helping women-owned companies successfully launch and advance their businesses. She serves as a Trustee of the Down Town Association in New York and as a Board Member of The Cap & Gown Club of Princeton University.

Charles Jones

Charles is a founding member and faculty of The Creating We Institute.

A lifelong student of human nature, Charles began taking psychology courses at a nearby university while still in high school. Upon graduating from the University of Michigan with a degree in philosophy of mind, Charles continued his study of human nature, spending a considerable amount of his time with cutting-edge thinkers in the ontology of language, somatic learning, psychosocial development, motivation, and attention.

In parallel with his ongoing study of human nature, Charles has worked as a consultant and coach in the areas of collaboration, leadership, and organizational culture change in Fortune 500 companies such as Capital One, Citibank, IBM, Johnson & Johnson, JPMorgan Chase, Motorola, Pfizer, and Sanofi-Aventis. Articles on his innovative approaches have appeared in Fortune Magazine, The Economist, and Leadership Excellence.

In 2008, Charles proposed a radical new theory of emotion based on well-defined relationships between psychological needs, executive attention, and affective states. Charles is now hard at work expounding the implications of this new theory for leadership development.

When he is not in front of clients or behind a computer screen, Charles can usually be found outside playing tennis, hiking, snowboarding, bodysurfing, or listening to live music with friends. He can be reached at cjones@strategicleadershipresources.com

Dale Kramer Cohen
President, DKC Resources

Dale Kramer Cohen is a visionary marketing executive with an outstanding record of building global businesses and brands by designing transforming experiences for her client organizations and their stakeholders. She has worked within the Financial Services, Health Care, Consumer Goods, Telecom and Technology industries, reframing how they see the world and their customers, defining brand truths, and coalescing their sense of purpose and growth into actionable initiatives.

Dale is President of DKC Resources (www.DKCre.com) and is a marketing strategist and growth catalyst who brings a depth of experience in developing new business strategies, defining valuable customer segments, and designing innovative customer-centric marketing solutions. Dale was chief marketing officer of a leadership development company dedicated to advancing executive and emerging women leaders and was a founding partner of Delphi Associates. She has worked with numerous Fortune 100 clients, including Citibank, Simmons Co., Textron, Cigna, Omnicom, Met Life, Xerox and AT&T.

A graduate of The Wharton School, University of Pennsylvania, Dale is President of PennNYC (www.PennNYC.org), the alumni association of NYC engaging 20,000 area alums. Identified for her leadership, Dale was named in Penn People Making History (http://www.makinghistory.upenn.edu/node/480). She is a member of The Creating We Institute (www.creatingweinstitute.com), a member of the Trustee's Council of Penn Women and a pro-bono strategist for the Make-A-Wish Foundation.

Jerry Manas

Jerry Manas is the author of Managing the Gray Areas and the international bestseller Napoleon on Project Management, which Kirkus Reviews called, "The ultimate case study in effective project management."

His work, which is at the crossroads of project management and organizational development, is frequently cited by management guru Tom Peters, and has been highlighted in a variety of publications, including Leadership Excellence, The National Post, The Globe and Mail, The Chicago Sun Times, and The Houston Chronicle.

Through his consulting company, The Marengo Group, Jerry focuses on the human side of project management, with a specialty in virtual teams. Using the principles of simplicity, engagement, and trust, he is passionate about helping leaders create energized teams that are aligned and focused toward shared goals.

Jerry is co-founder of the popular blog site, PMThink!, and a founding member of The Creating We Institute. He is also a founding member of Project Management Institute's New Media Council, as one of the leading influential voices in the online project management space.

Jerry can be reached at jmanas@marengogroup.com or on Twitter as jmanas. Visit his website at www.marengogroup.com.

Catherine Mullally

Catherine Mullally is the Executive Director of Susan G. Komen for the Cure in Los Angeles County. In this role, she leads all operations of the non-profit, including strategy, communications, fundraising, grants and education. Prior to taking on this role, she was founder, President & CEO of the CMC Group, LLC, a strategy and leadership communications consultancy based in New York.

Mullally's media career has spanned twenty-five years. She has held positions at Ogilvy & Mather and McCann-Erickson. She led the first commercial project for the Children's Television Workshop, then launched and successfully led a global packaged media business for nearly a decade for MTV Networks (Viacom). There, her businesses won over forty awards for excellence and generated billions in retail revenue. She was an original member of MTV's mentoring program, she championed a year-long anti-violence initiative for the creative teams, and served on the steering committee for both mentoring and diversity.

A founding member and faculty of The Creating We Institute, Mullally is a dynamic public speaker, with appearances ranging from seminars, panels, public presentations, radio and television. Her clients span many industries, from financial service to hospitality, and include start-ups and non-profits. She specializes in the creative alignment of business and values based brand strategy.

Brian Penry

Brian Penry has been influencing brands for nearly four decades. A consummate designer/illustrator, writer and brand strategist, his expertise and imprint are seen across a wide range of industries and media, from the arts, entertainment and licensing, to the corporate as well as non profit sectors—and increasingly, online. Brian's brand building contributed to Infinity Broadcasting's historic growth and success, and continued when Infinity partners, CBS and Viacom became his clients. He is often entrusted with popular brand icons, including Sega's flagship game character, Sonic The Hedeghog (44 million sold to date), and Carmen Sandiego, the acclaimed educational TV/multimedia series by Broderbund/PBS and The Learning Co./Riverdeep UK.

Brian's work has influenced the marketing, packaging identities and products of an even wider range of brands and organizations, from Sony, Campbell Soup and Disney/Touchstone to Patek Phillipe, Coca-Cola, Carnegie Hall, Moscow's Bolshoi Opera and Ballet, Special Olympics International, and Mount Sinai Hospital, to name a few.

Brian's clean, crisp style, love of color and typography, and meticulous attention to detail are evident in his work. He has written for Leadership Excellence, and is working on two books of his own. He can be found at: www.penrycreative.com

Whitaker Raymond

Whitaker Raymond ('Whit'), a Principal of LodeStar Leadership, is strategic leadership consultant and executive coach to senior leaders and their teams, and is a founding member of The Creating We Institute. He has worked with a diverse group of large and small corporations for over 30 years, and is a master facilitator of executive groups and projects where collaboration, consensus, shared focus and collective commitment are necessary to enable organizations to reach higher levels of functioning.

Over his career, he held senior positions at Merrill Lynch, Princeton Center for Leadership Training, and Cummins Engine Co. Formerly, as a Partner with LodeStar Associates, Inc, he consulted to senior teams building "high performance (organizational) systems" and strategic planning. He has coached hundreds of executives over the past 20 years and organized the in-house Executive Coaching program at Merrill. His external clients include Asea Brown Boveri, IBM, FMC, Fidelity, GE Capital, Herman Miller, Johnson,& Johnson, Kodak, and Merrill Lynch,. He is a graduate of Bowdoin College, and he received his Master's degree from Lesley University. He lives in Jersey City, NJ and Clifton Park, NY. He can be reached at:
whitraymond@comcast.net

Nancy Ring

Whether coaching individuals or teams, Nancy helps clients to design and implement their strategies by tapping into employees' strengths and personal objectives, thereby enabling them to perform at their best. Her work in individual professional development, team building, organizational development, and interpersonal communication includes clients from Fortune 500 and smaller companies, along with not-for-profit organizations in the U.S., Europe, and Asia. Nancy is a founding member of The Creating We Institute.

Prior to co-founding The Communication Partnership, Ltd. in 1990, Nancy was a director in the Organizational and Professional Development Department of P.M. Haeger & Associates, an association management firm in Chicago. In addition to coaching board members, she worked with clients on strategic planning, organizational and board development, volunteer management, training, and fundraising.

Nancy began her career as Executive Director of Common Cause in Michigan, where she lobbied state and congressional leaders, and was responsible for political organizing, media, and fundraising, along with board and volunteer development. She lives in Charlotte, North Carolina where she serves as a coach for MBA students at Queen's University's McColl School of Business, and on the Board of Directors of The Diversity Council of the Carolinas. Please contact her at nring@thecommunicationpartnership.com.

Nancy is a Licensed HeartMath Provider.

Cindy Tortorici

Cindy Tortorici is an Executive Consultant, Coach, and Entrepreneur who specializes in inspiring leaders to combine their passion and purpose to get results.

After a 25-year corporate career as a business strategist and executive for Nike Inc, Saks Fifth Avenue and May Company, Cindy followed her muse and created The Link For Women, LLC in 2004 in Portland, Oregon. 'The Link' is a community that connects and mentors women from many walks of life by providing executive consulting, coaching, multi-day seminars and events that provide knowledge to make informed decisions and inspiration to think beyond.

Cindy is a member of The Creating WE Institute www.creatingweinstitute.com and partners with The Hyatt Leadership Forum www.carolehyatt.com. She works with a cutting edge team of experts who support women to flourish in their 'Seat at the Table.' www.thelinkforwomen.com/mentor.asp.

In 2007, Cindy was named "One of the 100 Most Powerful Women in Town" by the NW Women's Journal. A year later, Cindy was honored as the "Volunteer of the Year" for Girls Inc. of NW Oregon where she is currently the acting Executive Director. Girls Inc. inspires all girls to be strong, smart and bold!

Cindy can be reached at cindy@thelinkllc.com. Visit her website at www.thelinkforwomen.com.

Louise van Rhyn

Louise is a founding member of Creating WE Institute. (www.creatingweinstitute.com)

Louise is a social entrepreneur and Organizational Change consultant based in Cape Town, South Africa. Most of her work is focused on contributing to 'strengthening the fabric of South African society' and fulfilling her personal mission to enable more people to live with joy and possibility. She is a founder and CEO of the Symphonia group of companies. (http://www.symphonia.net/home.htm)

Louise has more than 20 years of experience as a change leader and activist and has worked in the US, UK, many countries in Europe, Singapore, Australia and South Africa. She holds a BSc degree, a Masters of Business Administration (MBA) and a Doctoral degree in organizational change (DMAN) and works with business leaders to help them develop and implement change strategies.

She is also actively involved in Leadership Development (supporting leaders on their development journey). In addition to consulting, facilitating large group learning & organizational development processes and lecturing, Louise was a founding member and faculty of The Creating We Institute.

Josephine Washington

Josephine 'Jo' Washington is the Founder and President of Growth Resources International, LLC (http://www.growthresourcesintl.com) which is a best practice consulting firm specializing in human performance, leadership excellence and organizational transformation creating extraordinary results. She is also a founding member of Creating WE Institute.

Jo coaches and consults with people of organizations that are seeking guidance on how to achieve their destiny, purpose, and goals. Globally, she delivers incredible human development solutions for all levels of leadership for both profit and non-profit entities. Jo is highly sought after to provide her services including organizational transformation, executive coaching, leadership workshops, stress management, team coaching, management training, process design, strategic planning, stress management & retreat facilitation. Jo creates significant customer value by sharing her deep understanding of the human and business performance transformational challenges. The hallmark of her success lies in her ability to inspire individuals to embrace their unique talents, to optimize their performance and to reach for new horizons. Jo's clients often praise and especially recognize her for delivering real solutions, designed to sustained breakthrough performance results.

Jo has coached and consulted with many leaders in North America, Jamaica, Europe, South America, and Africa. She has earned a Masters of Education Degree in Counseling from University of Pittsburgh. Her professional certifications include the Licensed HeartMath Provider, National Corporate Coach, Business Process Design Engineer, Advanced Project Management, Facilitation Trainer, WorkPlace Big Five Profile, DISC and PDI 360° PROFILOR Assessments.

B Tools, Resources & Assessments

Judith E. Glaser

1. **Leadership Workshop on DVD:**

   The Leadership Secret of Gregory Goose: 7-minute animated film, Power Points, Facilitators Guide and Handouts; Powerful 3-6 hour session on Power-with Leadership and Co-creating. Also used for Diversity Training. Available on www.creatingwe.com or contact: jeglaser@creatingwe.com

2. **Assessment:** The DNA Assessment (web-based): Extraordinary diagnostic tool with predictive power to help leaders, teams, and individuals pinpoint what dynamics to shift in order to create healthy, thriving organizations.

   Uses: Culture Change, Leadership Development, Alignment and Re-alignment, Team Development, Setting Strategies for Success, Facilitating Co-Creating Conversations, and more. Comes in a 360 Assessment Format as well as a general Survey and Assessment format.

3. **HeartMath Certified Provider:** One-on-one Coaching for Individuals along with emWave tools and workbooks for developing coherence and handling stress. Contact: Judith E. Glaser (jeglaser@creatingwe.com)

4. **Special Issue:** Executive Excellence Creating WE Institute Special Edition: Brain, Brand and Energy

5. **Why Leaders Succeed, How They Fail:** Powerful document to give leaders insight into how they can accelerate their success rate in guiding their organization forward to achieve audacious goals.

6. **Partnering for Success:** Process for infusing new thinking and elevating mindsets to increase ability for Partnering in your organization

   Tools: The Gauge, Ladder of Conclusions; 10-10 Partnering

7. Innovation Workshop, Toolkit and/or Summit: powerful process for infusing Innovation into your organization

8. **Workshops:** (More descriptions found at www.creatingwe.com)

- Vital Conversations – Transforming Difficult Conversations
- Co-creating Conversations® Workshops – Shaping Relationships, Teams & Organizations
- Wisdom of the 5 Brains – Neuroscience of WE Workshop
- Working in Concert – Teambuilding Workshop
- Building High Performing Teams Workshop
- Coaching for Success Workshop – for Individuals, Teams, Peers
- Listening Benchmarks Workshop
- Leadership, Brand & Culture Scan Workshop – What drives your culture? How do you shape your culture for success?

Lisa Giruzzi

A Transformational Conversation with Lisa Giruzzi, DVD and Action Guide: Are you ready for a change? Are you interested in having the life you *really* want? This powerful and provocative program is designed to simulate being at a 'live' seminar. The DVD and Action Guide help you to create your own personal plan of action based on your strengths. Available at www.transformationalconversations.com or contact info@transformationalconversations.com.

Deborah Dumaine

1. **Giveaway:**

   Complimentary Document Analysis: Is your writing enhancing or harming your leadership ability? (For corporate teams only; maximum 20 pages.)

2. **Better Communications Workshops:** (Full descriptions found at www.bettercom.com)

   - Reader-Centered Business Writing™ (live or virtual)
   - Writing for Leaders™
   - Energize Your E-mail®
   - Bottom-Line Thinking
   - Creating Powerful Presentations
   - Write to Win Sales®
   - Reader-Centered Technical Writing™
   - Special-audience workshops
   - Basically Writing
   - Grammar You Meant to Learn®
   - Procedure Writing
   - Write Your Strategic Plan
   - Writing Constructive Feedback™
   - Writing for Administrative Assistants
   - Audit Writing™
   - Executive Overview
   - Train the Writing Trainer
   - Virtual Document Coaching

C Books

Lisa Giruzzi

- 31 Days to Transform Your Life: A Daily Action Guide to Increase Joy, Satisfaction and Fulfillment

Judith E. Glaser

- Creating WE: Change I-Thinking to WE-Thinking and Build a Healthy Thriving Organization
- The DNA of Leadership
- The Power of WE
- Leadership Secret of Gregory Goose

Bud Bilanich

- Straight Talk for Success
- 42 Rules to Jumpstart Your Professional Success
- Your Success GPS
- Star Power: Common Sense Ideas for Career and Life Success
- I want YOU...To Succeed
- 4 Secrets of High Performing Organizations
- Using Values to Turn Vision Into Reality
- Fixing Performance Problems
- Solving Performance Problems
- Leading by Values

- Supervisory Leadership and the New Factory

Jerry Manas

- Managing the Gray Areas (RMC Publications, January 2008)
- Napoleon on Project Management: Timeless Lessons in Planning, Execution, and Leadership (Nelson Business, April 2006)

Deborah Dumaine

- Write to the Top: Writing for Corporate Success
- Instant-Answer Guide to Business Writing: An A-Z Source for Today's Business Writer

D References

1. **Rule #4: Live in Your Heart Zone:**
   * HeartMath® is a registered Trademark of the Institute of HeartMath

2. **Rule #14: Think Small: Studies**
   * http://www.pmthink.com/2009/03/ideal-team-size-is-there-magic-number.htm;
   * http://www.bioteams.com/2006/01/13/the_maximum_team.html;
   * http://knowledge.wharton.upenn.edu/article.cfm?articleid=1501

3. **Rule#15: Consciously Contagious**
   * HeartMath research – demonstrates that 10' is the range of heart energy emitted from a person that can be felt by another

4. **Rule #17: Tell it Like it Is**
   Rule #32: Be Willing to Change Our Beliefs
   * Co-creating Conversations® is a Registered Trademark of Benchmark Communications, Inc. & Creating WE, Inc.

5. **Rule #28: Synergize Your Teams**
   * APPLY©: Growth Resources International, LLC Copyright APPLY Invitation © 2002

6. **Rule #39: Look at WE, Not Me**
   * Hub and Spoke Graphic Copyright © 2009 Beresford Partners, LLC

Write Your Own Rules

You can write your own 42 Rules book, and we can help you do it—from initial concept, to writing and editing, to publishing and marketing. If you have a great idea for a 42 Rules book, then we want to hear from you.

As you know, the books in the 42 Rules series are practical guidebooks that focus on a single topic. The books are written in an easy-to-read format that condenses the fundamental elements of the topic into 42 Rules. They use realistic examples to make their point and are fun to read.

Two Kinds of 42 Rules Books

42 Rules books are published in two formats: the single-author book and the contributed-author book. The single-author book is a traditional book written by one author. The contributed-author book (like '42 Rules for Creating WE') is a compilation of rules, each written by a different contributor, which support the main topic. If you want to be the sole author of a book or one of its contributors, we can help you succeed!

42 Rules Program

A lot of people would like to write a book, but only a few actually do. Finding a publisher, and distributing and marketing the book are challenges that prevent even the most ambitious of authors to ever get started.

At 42 Rules, we help you focus on and be successful in the writing of your book. Our program concentrates on the following tasks so you don't have to.

- **Publishing:** You receive expert advice and guidance from the Executive Editor, copy editors, technical editors, and cover and layout designers to help you create your book.

- **Distribution:** We distribute your book through the major book distribution channels, like Baker & Taylor and Ingram, Amazon.com, Barnes and Noble, Borders Books, etc.

- **Marketing:** 42 Rules has a full-service marketing program that includes a customized Web page for you and your book, email registrations and campaigns, blogs, webcasts, media kits and more.

Whether you are writing a single-authored book or a contributed-author book, you will receive editorial support from 42 Rules Executive Editor, Laura Lowell, author of '42 Rules of Marketing,' which was rated Top 5 in Business Humor and Top 25 in Business Marketing on Amazon.com (December 2007), and author and Executive Editor of '42 Rules for Working Moms.'

Accepting Submissions

If you want to be a successful author, we'll provide you the tools to help make it happen. Start today by answering the following questions and visit our website at http://superstarpress.com/ for more information on submitting your 42 Rules book idea.

Super Star Press is now accepting submissions for books in the 42 Rules book series. For more information, email info@superstarpress.com or call 408-257-3000.

Other Happy About Books

Blitz the Ladder

The purpose behind publishing this book is to provide the many young professionals entering the business world a realistic view of how business is done and what they can expect to encounter.

Paperback:$19.95
eBook:$14.95

DNA of the Young Entrepreneur

The book takes the reader on a journey through knowledge, attitudes, values, and actions that spell the difference between success and failure in starting and running a small business—or between running an enterprise on a business-as-usual level and pushing it to great success.

Paperback:$34.95
eBook:$24.95

They Made It!

Successful immigrant entrepreneurs share their inspiring stories. If you are fascinated by the Silicon Valley dream and the stories of people who shaped it, this book is a must read.

Paperback:$24.95
eBook:$14.95

42 Rules™ to Jumpstart Your Professional Success

42 Rules to Jumpstart Your Professional Success is a guide to common sense career development, entrepreneurial achievement and life skills.

Paperback:$19.95
eBook:$14.95

Purchase these books at Happy About
http://happyabout.info/
or at other online and physical bookstores.

A Message From Super Star Press™

Thank you for your purchase of this 42 Rules Series book. It is available online at: http://happyabout.info/42rules/creatingwe.php or at other online and physical bookstores. To learn more about contributing to books in the 42 Rules series, check out http://superstarpress.com.

Please contact us for quantity discounts at sales@superstarpress.com

If you want to be informed by email of upcoming books, please email bookupdate@superstarpress.com.

Additional Praise For This Book!

"These '42 Rules for Creating WE' supercharge our approach to leadership and provide accessible reminders of how to stay our best and most productive selves while helping those we work with to do the same. The lessons in this book are 'difference makers' and are equally pertinent to both our work and life pursuits."
Scott Hartl, President & CEO of Expeditionary Learning Schools

"Everyone talks about thinking outside the box. '42 Rules for Creating WE' gives us a springboard by challenging the old 'do-it-yourself' paradigm and shows how collaboration trumps competition! The stories from a myriad of writers provide a wonderful image of what could be if there was more 'WE.' This book should be given out throughout our educational system so that it is not so foreign when we come into the business setting."
Beverly Kaye, CEO/Founder Career Systems International, Co-author: *Love 'Em or Lose 'em: Getting Good People to Stay*

"With wisdom that could only have been cultivated and inspired through years of study and experience, '42 Rules for Creating WE' offers the reading audience a pragmatic and accessible guide for optimizing organizational performance and building thriving, WE-centric communities. A must read for leaders everywhere."
Scudder Fowler, CEO, Liminal Group

"This book is a 'must' for corporate, political and academic leaders. Strong productive teams and/or families are founded on respectful collaboration. 42 Rules of Creating WE is a pearl of collective wisdom providing powerful insights in 'how to' uncover those secrets quickly."
Rhonda Lee, President Mac + Lee CEO, Karma Threads

"The 'creating we' philosophy is a refreshing and candid perspective on how we can live more productive, meaningful and mutually enriching lives, both personally and professionally. The concepts of giving with no expectations of return, exertion of consistently 'positive' energy, true transparency in interactions, and eliminating the 'black/white' or 'right/wrong' approach to perspectives on decision-making, are just a few of the necessary tools for modern organizational success."
Dan Townsend, M.D.

"Most of us stick hard to our individual viewpoints and don't see the benefits of collectively developing programs and networks. Jane Hewson's approach to consulting—reflected clearly in the tenets of Creating WE institute and the messages from colleagues in 42 Rules—builds consensus and effectively moves the needle for business leaders."
John K. Halvey, Group Executive Vice President and General Counsel, NYST Euronext

"There is nothing more important than building consensus in a healthy and effective way. The viewpoints of The Creating WE Institute members, shared in 42 Rules, should be daily touchstones for all of us in leadership positions, no matter what kind of business we are in."
Lori M. Sackler, First Vice President, Senior Investment Management Consultant, Wealth Management Specialist, Morgan Stanley Smith Barney

"This is a power collection of strategies and techniques to assist anyone who knows the power gained by harnessing the best of people through effective collaboration."
Ronna Lichenberg, Co-founder and CEO, Virtual Coaching, and Author

"Principled negotiation requires a perspective that moves beyond compromise to a generative type of thinking, creating optimum solutions for all the parties involved. This cannot be accomplished or even conceived without first changing the win/lose mindset which is deeply ingrained in our thoughts about success.

In '42 Rules for Creating WE,' the authors share valuable information, experience and best practices for achieving powerful results while at the same time securing the well-being and creative, generative intelligence of people in organizations across the globe.

Olympic athletes depend on each other to push the limits of human capability. It is possible that as leaders and organizations commit to WE-centric thinking, we will move beyond the limits of what was previously thought possible in our world."
Mary Ann Somerville, Consultant and Executive Coach: Mobius Executive Leadership, Triad Consulting Group

"A well-arranged smorgasbord of tips and practices, each reliably designed to take your emotional intelligence and leadership effectiveness up a few notches."
Bill Joiner, author of Leadership Agility

"'42 Rules for Creating WE' provides simple and usable tools that encourage leaders to live the values of their brand. 'WE-centric' teams speak the same language, and use brand values as a filter for decision-making. Great leaders recognize it takes courage to lead from a WE-centric perspective, yet when they step into a 'WE-state of mind' they discover they are more fully equipped to make tough calls, and use their seat at the table to harness their brand values for 'across-the-board' success."
Michelle Lantow, CEO/President, Lucy Activewear

"We work and live in a fast-paced world where the rules keep changing! The '42 Rules for Creating WE' facilitates a much guided and inter-connected path, where we are able to find our humanity and creativity, to successfully navigate our way in the world."
Melanie Burke, Senior Program Director, Common Purpose

"Competition has always been a cornerstone of capitalism and the free-market system. The assumption has been that competition is geared towards competitors, not colleagues. This is frequently not the case. Creating organizations aimed at co-operative behavior was a first step but Judith Glaser has taken this concept to a different level. Through this book, she has invited a group of managerial and organizational specialists to share their unique insights into how people in organizations can contribute to effectiveness but also to individual, human fulfillment—while making good money."
Steven Naude, Pearson SA

"Judith has used her 'WE' philosophy to bring us a book which captures the very essence of what she believes in—essential extracts of thought and wisdom from a community of people, across an extensive network. Each page has at least a morsel to savor, some a full meal to digest. You are invited to sit at the table, join in the conversation or take away what you need."
Rhona Mears, Director, Symphonia UK

"We need WE. We all need this book. '42 Rules for Creating WE' is a beacon, reminding us to steer clear of the dangers, limitations, and false securities of I-centric thinking. Too often we fall blindly into status-quo, me-first, win-lose, and mechanical or hierarchical thinking. Too often we forget that we share common goals and aspirations, and that we are social by nature. Judith Glaser reminds us over and over again that work is social, that community is social, that we are social. WE-centric thinking provides a means by which each of us can exercise our skills and talent in service to shared intent. A WE-centric approach invites participation, calls for individual responsibility and action, and obligates teamwork and cooperation. Isn't this something we all want? We all

would do well to embrace the WE-centric perspective. In short, this book is a practical save-me-from-myself-yet-again guide to leading and living. "
Frank Lehner, Co-founder, The Ingenious Workplace

"'42 Rules of Creating We' swims against the tide of egocentrism that does *so* much harm in this world. The worst answer lies within a person, even worse it lies halfway between us. The ultimate, almost always, is found when great minds meet in a special way. 'The special way' is what it is all about and 42 Rules does it for us."
Van der Spuy Brink, Orator, Facilitator, Philosopher

"The biggest untapped lever in business today isn't strategy: it's organization and people development. Moving from 'me' to 'we' is the breakthrough concept. Companies, business leaders, and functional managers will achieve differentiated results by embracing these concepts. '42 Rules for Creating WE' is the playbook."
Bradley Bullington, Vice President, Corporate Strategy, Seagate Technology

"Whether you're a Special Operations warrior or a corporate warrior, The '42 Rules for Creating WE' can help you inspire your teammates—those you have to lead into battle. An excellent book for warrior-leaders who seek to dominate their chosen battle space."
Dick Couch, Special Operations Consultant & Author

"This compendium of rules to create effective teams provides expert guidance to all in their workplace and personal life. It confirms natural human responses to common workplace actions with recent studies in neuroscience. It is easy to read and even easier to apply. This book is a must read 'now' for everyone in the workforce."
Ed Steger, Life Coach

"Expressing appreciation, generating cooperation, and fostering an overall healthy and positive work environment are concepts that we all intuitively know to be instrumental to the success of any organization, be it a fortune 500 company or an elementary school. '42 Rules for Creating WE' eloquently transmits the know-how needed to convert this intuition to practical application, allowing leaders to take their organizations to levels which they would have thought unimaginable."
David Isaacs, The World Café Community Foundation

"No truer words have been written, especially in today's digital world: 'We are what we write.' From Deborah Dumaine's chapter on 'you' focused writing to other inspired yet practical advice, the team that assembled the 42 Rules did us a great service. They put everything one needs to create a wonderful organization under one cover. Kudos and thanks."
Michael L. Woodard, Director, Georgia Pacific University

"The Creating WE Institute has rediscovered age old wisdom, and has written a book that speaks to everyone. There is no more important than how the I and the WE engage."
Mike Jay, Author, Executive Coach & Developmentalist

Breinigsville, PA USA
31 December 2009
230017BV00004B/4/P